Stallions

Species-appropriate management and safer handling

STEFAN SCHNEIDER | STEFFI BIRK

Stallions

Species-appropriate management and safer handling

CADMOS

Exclusion of liability:
The authors and the publishing house reject any liability for accidents or damages of any kind that could result from the exercises, advice and opinions presented in this book.

Safety tips:
This book depicts people riding without hard hats and leading horses without wearing gloves. This is not recommended.
Always make sure that you have the appropriate safety equipment when dealing with horses and, in particular, stallions: boots and gloves for ground work and riding hat, riding boots and riding gloves for riding.

Publishing information:

Copyright ©2013 by Cadmos Publishing Ltd,
Richmond Upon Thames, UK
Copyright of original edition ©2012
by Cadmos Verlag GmbH,
Schwarzenbek, Germany
Translation: Helen McKinnon
Design: Ravenstein + Partner, Verden
Setting: Das Agenturhaus, Munich
Cover photograph: Christiane Slawik
Content photo: Birte Ostwald, Christiane Slawik
Unless specified otherwise
Editorial of original edition: Maren Müller
Editorial of this Edition: Christopher Long
Printed by: Westermann Druck, Zwickau

British Library Cataloguing in Publication Data
A catalogue record of this book is available from the British Library.

Printed in Germany
ISBN: 978-0-85788-012-3

Contents

Foreword

The legend of the stallion: the expression of passion, grace and masculinity. (Photo: Slawik)

Who isn't deeply moved by the sight of a stallion shining in the sunset as he gallops across a field or doesn't feel enthralled by the intense power that a stallion shows in his impressive movements? How many people are thrilled to read about famous stallions in the media, despite not being otherwise (horsey) themselves? Why do horses in their ultimate masculine expression fascinate so many cultures all over the world?

Horses' ancestors lived as long as 60 million years ago. Natural selection, which ensured their survival and led to their eventual development into our domesticated horses, made today's sires what they are: strong, highly evolved and capable of survival. They are remarkable performers who can not only survive in the human-dominated,

Arabians were given as gifts as a sign of affection and respect and are still admired all over the world today.
(Photo: Slawik)

noisy, busy world, but also captivate entire nations.

We hope that everybody who loves stallions will benefit from our many years of experience as trainers, stallion owners and vets and gain an insight into the world of these wonderful animals. This book explains typical behaviour and provides the reader with information about species-appropriate handling, management options, and important aspects of training, as well as basic knowledge about breeding. It is intended to be a reference book all about stallions.

Why **stallions?**

For as long as anybody can remember, stallions have been the epitome of strength, grandeur and elegance. Stallions catch the eye with their confident demeanour, shiny coats, alert, keen eyes and powerful, crested necks. It is hardly surprising, then, that there is a centuries-old tradition of stallion ownership in many parts of the world. Stallions have always been revered and used for breeding or given as a peace-offering and gift of reconciliation between different nations.

Purebred Arabians are a well-known example of this. People have been actively breeding them since as early as the seventh century and it is written in the Koran that purebred horses are covetable. Arabian rulers emphasised their eminence and social standing by owning the most powerful stallions that exuded the most masculinity. Giving an Arabian stallion as a gift is still seen as a sign of particularly high regard today.

For centuries, the Arabs ruled Spain and so the reputation of the Arabian horse, without which this dominion would not have been possible, spread to Central Europe. In the nineteenth century, noble houses sent out entire expeditions to secure a few Arabian horses. It is said that the Arabian horse is the source upon which nineteenth-century Europe drew to develop its modern, noble breeds of riding horse. The English Thoroughbred is also descended from the Arabian and, today, Arabian stallions are even used in Warmblood breeding to preserve and further develop the stamina, health, strength of character and affability of these horses.

Examples of how much stallions were and are valued can also be found in other cultures. In Spain, the stallions of the Pura Raza Española were considered to be the horses of kings and the white Lipizzaner stallions were originally bred for the imperial court.

Today, the Spanish Riding School in Vienna still only works with stallions. At events all over the world, you will mainly see stallions, because their noble appearance goes down particularly well with the public.

Hardly anyone can resist the fascination that stallions have always held for us. They still have cult status in the twenty-first century and the "legend of the stallion" is unbroken. Books and films such as "Black Beauty" and "The Black Stallion" are true classics and stallions act like magnets that draw crowds all over the world. Stallion shows at all of the famous studs regularly sell out and, at the moment, "century stallion" Totilas pulls in capacity crowds at international competitions.

But today, unfortunately, a great many stallions are no longer kept in order to pass on their qualities to progeny or to fully develop their potential for performance through appropriate training. All too often, people are seduced into buying a stallion by thoughts of prestige alone and only too soon many of these proud stallion owners come to despair of their impressive and powerful status symbol. It goes without saying that it is perfectly acceptable to choose a stallion as a leisure companion, providing that you can guarantee suitable handling and species-appropriate management. Anybody who wants to spend their time with stallions must be clear about the fact that stallions require much more from their owners than mares or geldings. The strength of the reproductive drive that, unlike in mares, exists in stallions all year round, day after day and that can override everything else, must not be underestimated. Stallion owners need to be experienced and knowledgeable horsemen and women in order to guide their horse in life and also to keep it on the right track. This book offers support for doing this.

As show horses, stallions enchant people all over the world. (Photo: Slawik)

The nature and behaviour of stallions

The natural order in the herd: the herd leader goes first and all of the others follow, with the last horse usually being the lowest-ranking. (Photo: Ostwald)

We want to begin this chapter by digressing into the nature of all horses. Basic knowledge about the behaviour and communicative ability of horses is the basis for dealing with them, irrespective of the gender of the horse in question, your preferred equestrian discipline or the breed you have chosen. This knowledge will make training easier for us in many respects: the descriptive examples below make this clear. And, with this background knowledge, it is also easier to understand and correctly categorise the typical stallion behaviour described in the rest of this chapter.

The **nature** of horses

Horses are herd animals and, as such, are dependent on other members of their species. In their natural environment, horses that have been excluded from the herd would generally be faced with certain death. Social isolation is therefore one of the worst punishments for a horse. We should obviously bear this fact in mind when managing in our day-to-day work with horses and, under some circumstances, you can take advantage of it during training. If we confidently work with a horse without the presence of other horses, the horse will bond with us during this time and will therefore no longer feel alone. If the horse now demonstrates unwanted behaviour, rudely barging over the top of us when being led, for example, we can let go of the lead rope and send the horse away from us with our body language. This is only an option if we are in an enclosed area such as an indoor school.

Horses are also flight animals. In the wild, their flight instinct is essential for survival, allowing them to flee from potentially deadly attacks by predators. Even when in the care of humans, horses cannot simply switch off this flight instinct, so they normally react with flight behaviour to situations that they perceive to be threatening, such as unidentifiable sounds or sudden movements.

The horse is startled by a stimulus from the left of the picture, so jumps to the right and raises his head so that he can better focus on the trigger. (Photo: Ostwald)

The horse's field of vision: the horse cannot see the red areas. It can see the green areas, which it perceives most clearly from a distance, with both eyes. It can only see the blue areas with one eye.

Horses often shy or spook when something happens in their immediate vicinity that they cannot categorise. They do have practically 360° vision (approximately 355°), but blind spots exist immediately in front of their front hooves, below their head and neck, as well as one to two metres right in front of their head. Furthermore, horses perceive a large part of their field of vision rather indistinctly and with just one eye. They can only see objects that are in the distance clearly. Last, but not least, they also lack spatial vision. Spatial vision only works in the relatively small area that they can perceive with both eyes. It is therefore not surprising that horses are wary of puddles or shadows, since, from their point of view, they could be deep holes.

In training, this means that you shouldn't punish a horse that is following its flight instinct. It is better always to keep a watchful eye on the environment yourself. If you notice a shadow on the ground, you can react before the horse is frightened by it. Furthermore, it is also possible to prepare horses for different situations and changes in their surroundings so that flight behaviour occurs less often or less severely.

The survival of a flight animal depends, among other things, on its reaction speed. This knowledge is useful to us in training, because horses have an extremely short reaction time. While it takes human beings around three seconds just to perceive and react to a stimulus in their environment, the reaction time of a horse is a mere three-tenths

to eight-tenths of a second. A horse is also only capable of associating a stimulus with a reaction if the reaction follows the stimulus within a maximum of three seconds. So, if a horse is only praised or punished for getting an exercise right or wrong after he has been ridden, he will not be able to make the connection. Praise or punishment therefore always has to follow immediately.

Horses like to conserve energy. in the wild, energy-rich food is in short supply. If horses do not need to run and also have no excess energy to burn from eating too much con-

centrate feed, they will instinctively avoid excessive movement. If flight is necessary, horses will only run a few hundred metres to begin with and then check whether the threat is still present or whether they can stop. If horses would run for several kilometres because of every "flight trigger", they wouldn't have enough energy left over for a real threat. When it comes to training, we have to remember that it is natural behaviour and not stubbornness that causes our horses to slow down once they have been expending energy for some time. First, we

In the wild, horses spend most of their day eating, which is the only way they can fill up with enough energy in their often sparsely vegetated habitat. (Photo: Ostwald)

must gradually teach horses that they have to work for longer periods at a time. It now also becomes clear why breaks in training are so important.

Horses are herbivores and in the wild they mainly eat low-energy plants and grasses. With a volume of just 18 litres, a horse's stomach is relatively small. For a horse to be able to meet its daily energy requirements, it has to eat for 14 to 18 hours a day (information varies depending on the source). As a result, evolution has given horses a great desire to chew that is still present in our domesticated equines. We need to take this into consideration when feeding and make plenty of roughage available. Adequate supplies of energy can be obtained with small quantities of rich, concentrated feed, but when the feed has all been eaten up, some horses start crib-biting, while others gorge themselves on straw and shavings or gnaw away at fences or stable walls. Gastric ulcers occur significantly more often where there is a shortage of roughage.

The daily routine in the wild

Wild horses living in a herd would spend the 24 hours of a day roughly as follows: 20 percent of the time standing still, sometimes dozing, 10 percent lying down and 10 percent maintaining social contact, for example in the form of mutual grooming, playing or play-fighting together. Horses spend the other 60 percent of the day constantly consuming food. Small groups kept in open barns, where hay and straw is freely available, behave in the same way.

Horse owners often accuse their animals of planning their behaviour, for example deliberately annoying them or being difficult to load because they "know" that it is time to go to the vet. But, unlike predators, horses are scarcely capable of thinking strategically. The part of the cerebral cortex that is responsible for this, the neocortex, is much smaller in horses than in cats, dogs, tigers or wolves, for example. In order to be successful, hunters have to plan their actions to a certain extent and success, i.e. killing the prey, is essential for a predator's survival. Horses, on the other hand, just lower their head to the ground and they either find food there or they don't. If there is nothing edible they will move on until they find something. Therefore, horses do not need a strategy to survive. They have neither to exert themselves particularly nor fight for food. Renowned horse trainer Monty Roberts once said on the subject:

"a blade of grass has never run away from a horse." This is also why a treat is less of a motivator for a horse than it is for a dog, for example.

But then how do horses think? They think in pictures. We can imagine this thought structure as being a little like a flick book. Behavioural researchers talk about "associative thinking" and the following example shows how this works in everyday handling: when out on a ride, the path leads by a rubbish bin. The horse shies at the bin and is reluctant to go any further. At this point, the rider uses his whip roughly to encourage the horse to walk on. Although it works in the end and they are able to pass the bin, the horse hesitates at the same point on the next ride. Why? The horse has made a connection between the pain of the whip and the image of the bin. It is the same with horses who keep suddenly running backwards out of the horse trailer after a specific point. Often, they have either banged their heads on the trailer at precisely this point or were "motivated" from behind with a broom the first time they didn't want to go forward.

Again and again, you can observe people trying to push horses around at their hip, shoulder or elsewhere to let other horses pass or to get more space, but the horse doesn't move. Instead, it braces itself against the pressure. This is a natural reaction called "opposition reflex" (colloquially also known as "into pressure"), which was discovered by Ivan Pavlov. Animals often instinctively orientate themselves towards pressure, whether they run along close to a fence, even though there is adequate free space available, lean into the contact when some-

The "opposition reflex" can be seen clearly here: the handler pulls to the left of the picture and, instead of yielding to the pressure, the horse resists it. (Photo: Ostwald)

body strokes their fur or pull backwards in response to someone pulling on their halter. This behaviour can also be useful for people, for example, when saddling a horse for the first time in its life. Thanks to the opposition reflex, the horse will normally stand still until you leave the "pressure zone" immediately around it (1.5 to 2 metres). However, you should not just be aware of this reflex in day-to-day dealings with horses; you can and should also teach them to yield to pressure. There is more about this in the chapter on training.

It should also be noted that wild horses neigh less often than our domesticated horses, because, in the worst case, loud neighing could attract predators. However, horses are not totally silent in the wild either. Mares neigh to their foals and vice versa. During mating, horses snort and squeal, and loud "screaming" is definitely part of a stallion's repertoire, especially when an adversary comes too close.

Loud whinnying is typical of our domesticated horses, but less common in the wild. (Photo: Ostwald)

Mares sort out pecking order in seconds. The higher-ranking mare reprimands the rival by flattening her ears and threatening. (Photo: Slawik)

Herd **structure**

People often talk about the so-called dominant stallion. In actual fact, while the stallion does occupy a certain position in the herd, as well as having specific duties, the herd, ranging up to 20 horses in size, is led by the dominant mare. She decides which mares the stallion is allowed to cover, which direction the herd takes and when and who may drink first at the watering place. She also teaches the young horses and leads the herd when they need to flee. The dominant mare is automatically the fastest, most alert and observant. Along with age and genetics, the individual experience and competence of the animal in question also play a role. For example, if the leader initiates flight too often without any actual threat being present, resulting in all of the animals wasting energy for no reason,

*Stallions discuss the "leadership question" in a
ritualised fight. (Photo: Ostwald)*

a "more competent" mare will automatically take over the leadership. In female animals, the process for establishing the pecking order usually only takes seconds, with mares using very clear gestures to show dominance or submission. It is often different with geldings and stallions, where there are many ritualised fights in which male animals playfully jostle for position. They rear at each other, bite each other's knees, squeal and threaten, but don't really hurt each other. Some horse owners will respond that they know many horses that have indeed been injured playing these games. The actual causes are usually lack of space, inadequate fencing, as well as unbalanced or insufficiently socialised horses.

But what role does the stallion play? The stallion is primarily responsible for reproduction and watches over his herd so that other stallions cannot "steal" his mares. During flight, he normally stays between his herd and the attacker and will defend the herd when necessary. However, fights are very rare, because flight is always the first strategy for horses and they will only fight in dire emergencies.

The herd structure described above is also known as a harem. So-called bachelor groups also exist. These herds consist exclusively of stallions and may temporarily be made up of up to 100 animals. The members are stallions who would otherwise have to roam alone, possibly because another stallion has stolen their mares. They find playmates in these groups and benefit from the protection that a herd offers. Bachelor groups are often also formed by the young stallions of one or more herds, because most of the colt foals born in a harem have to go their own way as soon as they reach sexual maturity. The dominant stallion will not tolerate any rivals that could mate with his mares, thus instinctively preventing any possible incest. However, a few low-ranking stallions remain in the herd and stallions of other herds may join if they do not make any move to compete with the dominant stallion. Only if the dominant stallion shows any weakness or even dies will one of the other stallions take over his position.

Bachelor groups wander around together as a herd until they are able to form a harem of their own. To form their own harem, horses either come together after leaving other herds or desert one stallion in favour of another.

Keep your distance!

If you observe a cohesive herd, either in the wild or in a field, you will see that, with few exceptions, horses always keep an individual distance from each other of at least 1 to 1.5 metres. They make exceptions when they come into close proximity to each other for mutual grooming, dozing head-to-head or in strong winds and severe weather.

During mutual grooming, horses enter what is normally each other's personal space. (Photo: Ostwald)

Stallion **behaviour**

We generally differentiate between innate and learned behaviour. Horses learn to stand up, suckle, run and neigh "in the cradle", so to speak. This behaviour can already be

Ritualised dunging: a stallion sniffs another horse's dung pile before covering it with his own. (Photo: Ostwald)

observed soon after birth. Behaviour that is necessary for coexistence with humans, such as lifting up the hooves in response to a signal or being led, first have to be learned through constant practice. But even species-specific behaviour, such as dealing appropriately with fellow equines, has to be learned to some extent, which is why it is so crucially important that horses grow up with other horses. A horse that has been hand-reared without equine company will find it difficult to communicate with other horses and will struggle to fit into a herd. It will not have learned the equine language of ear and nostril signals or the meaning of other body language cues, such as tail and head positions.

Much of equine behaviour can be observed in both genders. In the following, we want to focus on stallion behaviour in particular. However, we recommend that all horse owners, and stallion owners, read up on horse behaviour in general (see book recommendations in the appendix).

So, the behaviour described here is typical of stallions, but may also occur occasionally in geldings. After all, geldings were once stallions for a certain time and, during this time, learned behaviour patterns developed, at least some of which may remain, and to what extent depends slightly on how early or late the castration took place. In rare cases, even mares may show stallion behaviour and, conversely, there are stallions that do not show the behaviour that is actually typical for them. We are going to generalise because we cannot go into every peculiarity. Nevertheless, please remember that horses are individuals and that their repertoire of behaviour includes virtually

Flehmen: stallions can "taste" smells through Jacobson's organ. (Photo: Ostwald)

unlimited variations. There are so many observable gestures and facial expressions that the same action can look quite different in different horses.

Let's start with an unspectacular, but very interesting behaviour, defecate over. If a stallion goes into a field where other horses' dung is still present, he will almost immediately begin to sniff it thoroughly. He will then usually cover the pile with his own dung or urine. However, if there are piles of dung from many horses in a field, the stallion will not cover all of them, only certain ones. Stallions "read" the dung or urine of other horses like a newspaper. The odour not only tells them the gender of the animal that defecated, but also, for example, how healthy a possible contender is or whether a mare is ready for mating. So, with his own dung, the stallion conveys

Two young stallions practise mounting during play.
(Photo: Ostwald)

how fit, young and strong he is. Once he has covered the dung with his own scent, the stallion will normally turn around and sniff the pile that he has covered again, as if checking his message. For stallions in particular, ritualised dunging has the important function of clarifying hierarchy without conflict. In the herd, the dominant stallion has the right to mark all dung piles, some of which may have already been covered, after all of the other stallions. The other animals acknowledge the stallion's superiority by not dunging over these piles. If another stallion defecates on one of the piles anyway, there will often be a fight to establish pecking order.

Flehmen is regularly observed in connection with ritualised dunging. In flehmen, the stallion curls his upper lip back so that the gums and incisors become visible. The head is raised, the neck stretched out, the eyes rolled back and the ears held out to the sides. Flehmen is used in both genders to investigate an interesting, unusual or pungent odour more closely. It allows the scent to travel along the palate when the horse breathes in, in order to reach the vomeronasal or Jacobson's organ, which specialises in perceiving odours. Stallions will also perform flehmen in the presence of an in-season mare.

When a stallion smells a mare in season, he naturally develops an erection, whether or not he has already covered a mare. We can then see the fully extended and engorged penis. The erection is parasympathetically, i.e. involuntarily, controlled by the nervous system, just like the functions of most of the internal organs. Erections can still happen even after castration and many stallions become erect even without the presence of a mare. This is presumably a case of sexual lust without the appropriate object. In bachelor groups, we can also observe how one stallion mounts another as a result of this. Occasional letting down of the penis beyond the extent necessary for urination is also beneficial from the point of view of health, because it removes keratinised cells called smegma.

Some typical behaviour patterns can also be observed in what are known as ritualised fights. These fights are played out by young stallions and later used to establish pecking order and to fight over mares in season. The mark of a ritualised fight is that both parties usually come out of it unscathed or, at the most, with minor injuries. These fights follow a certain pattern and the horses always exhibit the same behaviour during the fight, as described below.

Young stallions, in particular, will often mount each other. This has nothing to do with them being sexually attracted to the other stallion. Instead, they use play to practise accurate mounting from the side or from behind so that later they can immediately hold onto the horse they have mounted securely and without slipping off, at the first attempt. Furthermore, they use this behaviour to signal certain dominance over the horse they are mounting.

Stallions also "dance" with one another. Admittedly, this is expressed in very human terms, but it really does resemble a couple dancing. Two stallions rear up facing one another and support themselves on their hind legs with their forelegs on their counterpart. In order to keep their balance, they have to make small sidesteps with their back legs that look like dance steps. While standing up in the air like this they now try to nip or bite each other on the throat, neck, chest or shoulder.

Horses can also bite each other with all four feet on the ground. To do so, two stallions stand close together while facing in opposite directions and try to nip each other on the front legs or groin. Because each is avoiding the bites of the other, they begin to circle. It can even get as far as both stallions nipping each other on the knee until they end up kneeling down. When we talk about biting here, we do not mean

The "dancing" stallions use their front legs to support
themselves against each other. (Photo: Ostwald)

tearing off great chunks of skin, but nipping or pinching with the teeth. Normally, a little hair is bitten off now and then at the most. Some stallions also perform a kind of boxing. They stand on their hind legs facing each other and then each strike out in the direction of the other horse with their front legs. Again, they are improving their ability to use their individual limbs accurately.

Constant movement can be observed in a herd. Either one horse follows another or it is moved by another, usually hierarchically superior, horse. The dominant horse drives the other horse away by walking forward with a threatening, usually slightly lowered, head and flattened ears. As they do so, stallions often actively use their head to shove against their opponent's head, neck, shoulder or belly. This enables them to accurately steer a member of the herd and therefore express their higher ranking position. In states of high excitement and to make an impression, stallions, and sometimes also riggy geldings, also show very typical patterns of behaviour. This includes prancing on the spot, similar to a piaffe in dressage,

A stallion drives other horses away with flattened ears and a slightly lowered head. (Photo: Slawik)

High excitement is expressed by a raised tail, flared nostrils and tension in the whole body. (Photo: Ostwald)

that can change into a floating trot (passage), depending on the situation. The head and tail are carried high, the nostrils flared, and loud snorting and trumpeting can be heard. When a stallion exhibits this behaviour, it can be extremely difficult to control him or to get his attention back, because he is often in a kind of trance at this moment. He no longer perceives the handler and his surroundings, but focuses solely on the trigger for this behaviour. If the horse is out in the field, he will quickly calm down again by himself. However, if you are riding or leading the stallion, you should ride or lead him in lots of circles to regain his attention or to keep yourself out of danger. When leading from the left you should favour a left circle over a right circle. That way, there is less risk of you being run into and knocked over by a highly excited horse

and it is also very difficult to "push" a horse away from you when it is in this state.

To impress mares, stallions also stand with their head held high and all of their muscles tensed and paw or stamp powerfully with their front hooves.

When they meet a new horse for the first time, stallions sniff at the newcomer's genitals, regardless of whether it is a stallion, a gelding or a mare. This, again, tells them about fertility, phase of cycle, strength and health and so we return to the ritualised dunging described at the beginning.

Showing off: arching the neck and stamping the front feet. (Photo: Ostwald)

To conclude this chapter, we would like to consider a possible behavioural problem in stallions. Some stallions gradually develop ever-increasing aggression, which may be directed at mares that the stallion is going to mate with or at people. These stallions bite, kick or rear and sometimes even direct this aggressive behaviour against themselves. This problem often arises in breeding stallions that have insufficient social contact with other horses once they start servicing mares, are only taken out of their stable for covering and are bored or under-stimulated. It is also seen in stallions who are incorrectly handled or who haven't been reared properly. Aggressive behaviour caused by a genetic predisposition is possible, but very rare. However, this cause is difficult to verify and misinterpretations are common. If the offspring of a stallion behaves just as aggressively as the progenitor, the behaviour could also be down to the same imbalance and unsuitable management. It does not necessarily have to have been inherited.

Displacement activities

Other behaviour that has not been described above but that can be relevant to horse owners can be observed in all types of horses and therefore also in stallions. This behaviour is known as "displacement activity". We would like to address displacement activities briefly at this point, in order not to leave readers completely alone with unknown behaviour as they observe their stallions. Displacement activities are compensatory movements made by the horse that are not related to the current situation. An example would be a stallion that bites the rope or post in front of him because he is tied up short, instead of biting at his belly or the rider as he objects to the constraint of the saddle when being tacked up.
We recommend observing any behaviour closely in order to establish the possible cause of displacement activities.

Managing stallions

After successful training, stallion and rider can enjoy public events without stress.
(Photo: Ostwald)

There are a few things to keep in mind if you own a stallion and deal with him every day. How easy or difficult the stallion is to handle in everyday life admittedly depends on character and temperament, as it does with any horse, but there are also a few fundamental things you should emphasise when rearing and training stallions, in comparison with mares and geldings. In this chapter, we present training goals that stallions should achieve gradually under human guidance. We will also go into handling the mature stallion at public events and explain how both stallion and handler can achieve positive results.

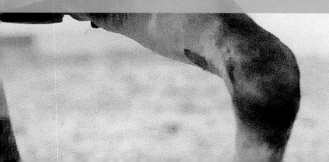

It shouldn't look like this. Work on basic training is urgently required here. (Photo: Ostwald)

Although every stallion owner's goal should be to rear and train his or her horse in such a way that it can be controlled at all times, dangerous situations cannot always be avoided. That is why we also want to dedicate a few pages at the end of this chapter to "crisis management".

What makes mares, stallions and geldings **different?**

To begin with, we want to look quickly at the differences that exist between the sexes when it comes to training. However, we have to start by saying that "trainability" does not depend on gender alone, but also on a horse's status. In this respect, we can distinguish among three groups. Horses in the first group have a dominant position in the herd. They are mainly mares, but there may also be male horses. These horses are rather reluctant to give up their leadership and we humans need to handle them with great consistency if we are to take over leadership in the long term. The second group consists of horses who are lower in the pecking order but nevertheless still regularly challenge the dominant animal, albeit unsuccessfully. They are not quite as challenging to handle as horses in the first group, but you must still expect them constantly to call your leadership into question. The horses in the last group are the easiest to handle because they, also known as "hangers-on", are the lowest ranking. They are neither ignored nor chased nor bitten by the other members of the herd. They are simply always there and appear to go along with everybody. This type of horse is ideal for less experienced owners or anybody who does not want to be constantly challenged when dealing with their horse.

Now let's move onto the actual differences between the genders. It is apparent that mares question their trainers and try to take over the lead more often. This behaviour probably stems from the fact that mares, as described above, often take the lead in herds. So, if the trainer is inattentive or reacts inappropriately to a situation again and again, the mare will take over the leadership. She will do it without any major conflict, just as she would in the herd. Thankfully, the mentality of "elbowing each other out of

the way" does not prevail among horses. A mare who does not feel safe and protected will inevitably protect herself if need be by breaking away and running back to the stable. Many mares remain fundamentally more wary and sceptical and are more watchful than male horses. Of course, mares are also influenced by their cycle. When they are in season, mares are often much more sensitive physically and sometimes react more aggressively than when they are not in season. From a human point of view, they can be really "touchy", which can be seen, for example, when they suddenly act defensively towards their otherwise tolerated stablemate (by kicking the stable wall or threatening through the bars) or kick out when having their feet picked out, simply because the owner accidentally touched their belly.

Things are a little different with stallions. In herds, they tend to squabble with one another and measure their strength in ritualised fights. Young stallions, in particular, but also incorrectly reared mature stallions, try to show this behaviour towards humans. Typical behaviour includes trotting past the handler when being led, snapping in the direction of the rope or hand or even deliberate rearing against the person. Utmost consistency is required here to nip any attempts of this kind in the bud. Making the horse move backwards from the ground is an appropriate measure. If a stallion rears under saddle, for example, riding forwards briskly or riding circles will help, because it will make it impossible for the horse to rear. In both cases, the horse has to keep working, which is unpleasant for him because he is an "energy saver". Under no circumstances should this type of behaviour be followed by a break for the horse, because the horse will interpret it as a reward.

Imagine a stallion who, as a foal, tried to mount his owner or who kicked out to the front or back to make room for himself.

This may look cute in the little chap, but should under no circumstances be regarded as "normal stallion behaviour" that he will "soon grow out of". Looked at realistically, the boisterous little stallion is a rebel who needs to be cut down to size. Otherwise he

A relaxed team who are well attuned to each other.
(Photo: Ostwald)

will still exhibit the same behaviour as a considerably taller three year old and that is not a pleasant prospect. It is clear that there is greater potential for risk with a stallion than with a mare. While we can possibly turn a blind eye with mares every now and then, this should never be done with stallions under any circumstances.

However, the advantage of a stallion compared with a mare is that, once the relationship has been unequivocally clarified, he will normally stop questioning it. So, if you are very consistent from the outset and show the stallion his boundaries, you will end up with a great partner who can easily be controlled, even in difficult situations.

Now that we have looked at mares and stallions, geldings can be described very briefly. They were once stallions and may still show the stallion behaviour that they learnt in their youth to a certain extent after castration. However, they are almost always easier to handle because of the altered hormonal balance. Compared with mares, they take the lead much less often and they are not as moody.

Raising a stallion

In their most natural state, horses grow up in a herd. While a herd of stallions of the same age grazing on remote pasture may be a lovely image, the better choice is a herd of older stallions/geldings and young stallions. In a herd like this, the young stallion can test things out and learn the rules necessary for establishing a hierarchy. It is also important that, despite keeping a horse in a herd, care is still taken to ensure that it remains trusting, knows people and can be caught at all times. This avoids stress and conflicts and greatly simplifies the subsequent relationship between the owner and the stallion. If, on the other hand, a stallion grows up only among others of his own age, he will develop a lot of rather pronounced stallion-ish and showing-off behaviour because of the numerous scraps. If contact with people is lacking too, the young stallion also cannot learn that this behaviour is not acceptable when dealing with humans, which can make subsequent training more difficult and protracted.

Rearing horses in mixed herds

Many breeders allow colt foals or weanlings to run in large, mixed herds. This usually does not pose a problem, as long as the young stallion hasn't yet reached sexual maturity and none of the mares comes into season. Unfavourable effects can be expected if the stallion still remains in the herd after reaching sexual maturity and, either because of carelessness or perhaps even with breeding in mind, covers all of the mares in the field that are ready to mate. Pronounced stallion behaviour that has been acquired in this way makes training more difficult and will also remain after castration, which is often done when it turns out that the stallion cannot be graded.

Young stallions that grow up in a herd can test things out and learn the rules of cooperation in play fights. (Photo: Slawik)

In our opinion, the aim of a stallion's basic training should always be to be able to guide him with light aids. The sooner the necessary training begins, the easier and more fun it will be and the longer its effect will last, providing that what is learned is not forgotten in subsequent handling but is refined even further. This requires absolute consistency from the trainer. Of course, that applies to horses of either gender, but it is even more important for stallions because of their immense power and the control their impulses exert over them. A break can normally follow a phase of consistent basic training; for example, a break could mean that the young stallion spends a while turned out with other horses. Later, you can build upon the basic training you have already established. Changing to an inexperienced trainer with lax handling would be a bad alternative in all cases.

There is nothing wrong with teaching a stallion manners while he is still a foal. The first halter-leading exercises can be done with foals when they are just a few days or weeks old. These exercises are not about steering the foal in a certain direction or even leading him away from his mother. Instead, the aim should be to get the young stallion used to being haltered and to the associated movements, i.e. walking up to him and touching his body, neck and head. The next step is the first leading exercise with the halter and rope. To do this, the mare is led a short distance away by a helper. The foal will follow her (either immediately or after a short time, depending on his age and level of independence) and the trainer simply walks with the foal without using the halter to interfere with or correct the young stallion. This way, the young horse learns that the person walking by his side is not a threat. The mare is halted and the foal will copy his mother. The signal "whoa!" can be established by gently pulling on the halter just as the foal is stopping. If the helper starts walking forward with the mare again and the foal walks too, the trainer can also pull gently on the halter in a forward motion. If this training is repeated on a few consecutive days, the foal will learn to be led, step by step. One exercise session should not last for longer than five to ten minutes because foals can only concentrate for very short periods of time.

You can't teach an old dog ... a foal learning how to be led. (Photo: Slawik)

Warning

Foals still have soft cartilage and bones as well as growth plates that have not yet fused, so tugging and pulling on the halter may lead to irreparable damage!

It is important to habituate young horses to human contact all over their bodies, from the very start. Contact must always be made on both sides because horses only have a limited ability to transfer events that happen on one side of their bodies to the other side. It is best also to start working on briefly picking up all four hooves at this point.

Habituation to contact should only be done on a few consecutive days, after which there must be a break. From then on, the exercises can be integrated rather incidentally into daily handling at intervals of a few days or weeks. However, please always keep in mind that young horses should develop freely and that they have to learn their own language first, before people ask anything more of them.

At weaning age (from the seventh to the ninth month) you can begin to teach the young stallion to be led away from his mother and the herd, alone. He should also learn to move forwards and backwards on command (gentle pull on the halter and possible use of voice) and to follow the trainer around to the left and right. Voice commands that the horse learns to associate with a certain exercise, such as halting ("whoaaa!") can be useful. However, we should always remember that horses communicate non-verbally, i.e. silently, by nature and that sounds and words actually have no meaning for them. You should not rely on voice commands alone, because horses can only perceive their environment to a limited extent in extreme situations, making sounds useless. It is therefore much more important

A horse that has been startled and tries to run away will scarcely react to a voice signal. Standing upright in front of and to the side of the horse, with your arm raised, acts as a better brake. (Photo: Ostwald)

that the horse learns to respond correctly to the owner's body language and non-verbal signals (the pull on the halter, for example). If the horse gets a fright and wants to run away, it will perceive and accept a person standing in front of it and slightly to the side, with their arms raised, much more clearly as a signal to halt than it would a voice signal.

It is also important to consider the horse's reaction time. The horse can only associate a person's reaction with a previous action if it follows within a maximum of three seconds. For example, if you want your horse to stand with his head level with your shoulder when he halts, but your horse keeps walking for two more steps, it can be useful immediately to move him two steps back again. If you only do it after a time, the horse will not understand the connection. The following also applies here: body language should remain relaxed, with the shoulders loose, as long as the stallion is walking quietly alongside the handler and standing in sync with him or her. As a clear signal for the horse to move backwards, the handler stands more upright and turns to face the horse.

Backwards, but straight!

The horse's head must be straight to stop him from walking backwards diagonally. If the horse's head is facing to the left when he walks backwards, the quarters will swivel to the right. It is like reversing a car and trailer.

You should always establish right from the start where your horse is supposed to walk when you lead him. With his head a little bit in front of you? Or right next to you? Or even behind you, so that he can't overtake? As a stallion owner, you should be mindful of the fact that a horse is more difficult to control the further ahead of the handler he is. However, it can be dangerous to have a horse walking behind the handler, especially if the horse is a stallion. If the horse is a mature stallion actively used for breeding and somebody suddenly leads a mare out of the stable next door, the situation may become perilous for the handler if the stallion rears up right behind them. It is best to lead stallions, in particular, so that their head is level with the handler's shoulder. It is also important to make sure that you have enough "personal space" when leading the horse. For example, stallions can be very pushy towards menstruating women and in this situation it is also helpful if the stallion has learnt to keep his distance from the beginning.

The aim of halter training is that the stallion learns to accept that we determine the speed and direction, just as the highest-ranking horse in the herd would. We offer the stallion protection and security with our consistent behaviour. We take over the responsibility so that our horses can feel at ease around us. The foundations for a trusting partnership have been laid.

The basic training of a young stallion is about more than just leading. He should also become familiar early on with the many other things that he will encounter in his life as a ridden horse. For example, it is useful

The rein is loose, the stallion keeps his distance and his head is level with the handler's shoulder.
(Photo: Ostwald)

When asking him to move backwards, the handler turns to face the horse.
(Photo: Ostwald)

for the stallion to learn to have his feet picked up when he is a foal, starting with just a short while for picking out and then longer, so that he will not have any problems when the farrier comes. Step-by-step familiarisation with the touches, the smell of burning horn and everything else that can be expected from a visit from the farrier will ensure that everything is relaxed from the first shoeing or trimming onwards. The same applies to habituation to rugs, the snaffle bit in the mouth, loading and many other things. If the stallion becomes used to them at a young age and in a relaxed atmosphere, it is a solid starting point for owner and horse.

Suitable aids

Even though we do have our favourite training styles, we want to leave everybody to decide on their own method, rather than making any special recommendations. The most important thing is that you can use the equipment you are working with accurately and safely. If this is not the case, it is best to leave the training of the young stallion to a professional or to practise with an older, experienced horse until you can work safely.

There is a wide variety of different types of halter whose effects we would like to briefly explain here. The one thing that they all have in common is that they exert pressure. In the case of a normal head collar, the pressure is spread very extensively over the poll. Depending on the direction of the pull, pressure can be exerted on the side of the head or on the bridge of the nose, but it is very difficult to influence where exactly the pressure is exerted. When used for leading stallions it is often combined with a stallion chain. The stallion chain can be buckled either over the nasal bone or underneath the head a few fingers' widths above the chin. When using the second version, you should remember that muscles, tendons, nerves and the blood stream run under the chain. Pain will result if too much pressure is exerted.

A knotted halter made from thin rope tends to exert pressure at the poll, but with the difference that the pressure is more precise. Furthermore, pressure is exerted by the knots located on the left and right, as well as at eye level and also at the sides of the nasal bone, depending on the direction the halter is pulled. Correct fastening is very important with this type of halter. Depending on where the knots are located, it can be uncomfortable for the horse, especially as the halter fits very loosely and can slip easily when pulled. You should therefore make sure that the knots are positioned exactly as described above. Under no circumstances should the halter be fastened so low down that the noseband can slip down over the nose.

Dually halters, Geitner halters, stallion chains and correctly fastened cavessons run over the hard part of the nasal bone, which is also where they primarily exert their influence. In this area, there is only bone beneath the skin, so this part of the horse's head is relatively insensitive to pain. These different types of halters or cavessons have to be adjusted and fitted very carefully. They must not be so tight that they dig in, but also must not be so loose that they slip to the side and into the horse's eye when pulled. Nor must they be fastened too far down or the pressure will no longer be exerted on the bone but on tissue that is better supplied with blood and contains many nerves. The benefit of these aids is that pressure is released as soon the handler stops pulling on the halter. For successful training, it is crucial that pressure applied can immediately be released again as soon as the horse behaves correctly. This is the only way the horse can learn which behaviour represents the path of least resistance.

Special stallion head collars, which consist of a head and nose piece that are normally made from leather, are also available. An integrated chain under the jaw holds the two pieces together. Pressure is exerted on the chin groove when this chain is pulled. These head collars are often used at shows because they flatter the appearance of the head and they are most commonly seen on Arabians. However, they are made from very delicate material, the durability of

A correctly fastened cavesson, shown here with a bit.
(Photo: Ostwald)

A normal head collar with a correctly fastened stallion chain ...

... and a Dually halter.
(Photos: Ostwald)

which could be doubtful in emergencies. A stallion chain combined with a normal head collar does the same job.

If you do not use a stallion chain for leading, we recommend that you use a lunge rein or a rope of around three metres long. Compared with a normal two-metre-long rope, the longer lead rope offers the advantage that you have more room to manoeuvre, especially with an uneducated stallion, and that he cannot escape as easily in the event of any "antics". However, the opposite is also true, in that the risk of accident/injury increases with the length of the rope or lunge rein, should the horse nevertheless manage to get away from the handler. That is why it is important that the handler can work with these aids safely.

The material should be non-slip and not too thin. A high concentration of artificial fibres is not recommended because serious injury can result if the horse pulls the rope through your hand. To prevent this from happening, it is recommended that you always wear gloves when working with horses. Elasticated ropes or halters are also not recommended, because they just "dilute" signals.

Some trainers also use a whip to give signals, along with the halter and rope, which is, by all means, acceptable. The horse has to learn that tapping on the chest means move backwards or touching the flank means more activity in the hindquarters. The whip must be used accurately and as gently as possible. Under no circumstances must it be misused to hit the horse as punishment.

Basic training of the stallion

The chapters on rearing stallions and their basic training overlap on a few things, because some things are useful as a foundation but are only approached in basic training, for example preparation for the farrier, rugging or bitting. The more things a horse becomes familiar with early on, the more easily he will overcome future challenges. The saying "you can't teach an old dog new tricks" isn't quite true, but learning is definitely easier for horses in their younger years, which makes teaching easier for people. Some advice at this point is that horses not only have a short reaction time, they also learn very quickly. If the timing is right (i.e. if consequences such as praise or punishment come at the right moment), one to three repetitions are enough for a horse to understand something: picking up the feet, being tacked up, standing even though the gate to the field is open are all learned quickly. However, bucking, biting, kicking and rearing are established just as fast. If a horse manages, for example, to drive a person out of the stable by threatening them,

he will learn that he is then left in peace and will keep demonstrating this behaviour. The same goes for a horse who has managed to pull a treat out of a person's pocket. He will keep on trying, even if the pocket is empty. In the worst case, the handler will end up being bitten. Naturally, this kind of "bad behaviour" can be corrected but why train away tiresome habits when you can avoid them from the outset and focus on correctly training the desired behaviour? It is essential that you keep this in mind during basic training.

Tip: Staying relaxed at the vet's

The stallion should be habituated to veterinary treatments as part of basic rearing and, at the latest during training. This includes injections into the muscles or veins, being listened to with a stethoscope, flexion tests on all four legs, eye examinations, dental examinations, temperature measurement, oral administration of wormers and much more. Taking the horse's temperature or listening to his heart is very easy for the owner to replicate, but you can also practise injecting by pressing on the jugular vein with your thumb until the blood visibly accumulates or pinching a small fold of skin on the neck and "pricking" it with a pen or pencil. Horses who stay relaxed while they put up with this usually accept a real injection by the vet.

Even stallions need to be able to wait and to stay calm as they do so. (Photo: Ostwald)

With regard to breaking in a stallion, there are, again, many approaches that we do not want to look at in detail here. However, as with raising the foal, it is important that the horse's nature is taken into account and that the trainer can safely cope with the methods and equipment used. If this is not the case, it is better to leave the sensitive subject of breaking in to a professional, because accidents happen all too often during incorrect attempts at backing, which, in the worst case, puts human life at risk and also leads to long-lasting, perhaps even untreatable, trauma in the horse concerned. By way of an example, there are horses who will no longer allow themselves to be saddled because they were terribly frightened by a saddle that slipped under their belly and perhaps even fell over as a result or because they were not properly used to the saddle, reared and then toppled over in a bid to free themselves of the "predator" on their back.

However the stallion is broken in, a few goals should be achieved afterwards: the stallion should stand quietly when being saddled and bridled, and stay relaxed when being led into the indoor school or arena where he allows the rider to mount safely without spooking or running away. He should understand all of the weight, rein and leg aids, i.e. he should have steering, brakes and be able to be ridden in a controlled manner in the three basic paces. For further work, it is then important to get the stallion used to the idea that other horses, of either gender, may be in the vicinity during all exercises and activities but that he must not lose his focus on the rider. To begin with, there should not be too many mares in the arena and it is best to avoid riding directly behind a mare.

On the whole, you must keep in mind that stallions are enormously attracted to mares in season, so that even a well trained stallion may forget his good manners at the sight and scent of a lady. If this happens, it is

The rider has the stallion well under control. He is allowed to look at the other horse, but remains completely calm. (Photo: Ostwald)

Two stallions on the way from the warm-up area to the performance of "Classic meets Doma Vaquera". (Photo: Ostwald)

important to keep the stallion occupied with varied exercises when being ridden and to keep a good distance away from the mare. Controlled and foresighted riding prevents unpleasant incidents.

The stallion also has to get used to other horses arriving later and leaving earlier, while he is still being ridden. When work is finished, it should be possible to wash the stallion off with the hose without problems and loading onto a trailer or lorry should be a matter of course, not just for competition horses.

The stallion at **public** events

Nowadays there is a comparatively wide range of public events where stallions can take part. These include sports events in the form of competitions or races, stallion shows and stallion parades, as well as many and varied horse shows or even events with direct contact with crowds of people, such as carnival processions.

Not every stallion will remain quiet and composed in these situations. Temperament

Thanks to thorough preparation, this stallion has performed calmly and confidently. (Photo: Ostwald)

and character will play as much of a role here as basic training and careful habituation to everything that could await a stallion in a strange environment. It is very important that handlers can accurately assess their stallions and their possible behaviour and that they have sufficiently prepared them for all the hustle and bustle. Otherwise there is a risk of some unpleasant and downright dangerous surprises. Admittedly, mares and geldings can also cause difficulties in unfamiliar situations, but a stallion out of control poses a considerably greater danger to his environment. We want to go into possible problems and management of tricky situations later but before that, we want to look at avoiding problems.

Safe preparation

It goes without saying that it is possible to habituate horses to the hubbub of events and any other possible occurrences and to train them so that they still remain controllable even in unfamiliar situations. The principle is simple: you think about what the stallion could encounter at an event and then confront him with the corresponding stimulus under controlled circumstances to begin with. It is important to build things up slowly, which means only going to the extent where the stallion can still tolerate the stimulus and remain controllable. You should only progress on to the next step when he stays relaxed at low stimulus intensity. This results in step-by-step desensitisation. The benefit of this kind of training is that the owner learns how to judge his or her stallion better. What things does he meet where he responds with calm from the outset, what frightens him and how quickly does he calm down? A practical example exercise would be that the stallion should learn to remain calm and controllable in the presence of mares. Meeting mares is unavoidable, especially at events, whether it is in the collecting ring, on the way to the class or even in the stable next door. It is essential that you prepare a stallion for this situation before you leave the normal environment with him, especially if he mates with mares but otherwise does not come into contact with them or generally displays very stallion-like behaviour. Anything else would be grossly negligent. To begin with, it is enough to lead a mare, preferably one that isn't in season, past the stallion. It is up to the individual to decide whether the stallion should be standing in his stable or in the field or being ridden or led in the arena while the mare is led past. Gradually, other mares are added who will remain in the vicinity of the stallion for longer and longer. The aim should always be for the ridden or led stallion to be relaxed and able to be handled in the immediate proximity of several mares.

In general, it makes sense not to exclusively train the stallion by himself, in the peace of the early morning or late evening, but at busier times too. That way, he will automatically get to know many things that could also come his way at events, such as the presence of other horses or people or dogs or umbrellas, tarpaulins and much more. In brief: the more different stimuli the better, but not all at once of course!

Taking the stallion to small events without him taking part is a good additional preparation. This allows him to become familiar with the new situation without the pressure that would be unavoidable if he were taking part. The situation is also relaxed for the handler. You only need go as far as to allow the situation to remain calm and controlled and you can avoid risks. After all, all training, whether it takes place at home or away, should always end on a positive note. Taking the stallion to events also gives an indication of how training is actually progressing. What is already working well and what do you have to work on more at home?

Umbrellas and coloured blankets could be part of an "obstacle course". The stallion examines the strange objects with quiet curiosity. (Photo: Ostwald)

The "obstacle course" – training for the advanced

When training of individual situations is going well, you can specifically prepare the stallion for potential extreme situations. To do this, you need to build an "obstacle course", i.e. a kind of "ghost train" that the stallion has to complete in an indoor arena or in a fenced, secure area with the support of a few helpers. Here is an example:
When the rider crosses X, a mare will be led or ridden along the track at A. After a cross-pole at B, somebody opens an umbrella or holds up some balloons. Somebody else then pulls a large plastic tarpaulin behind them from left to right.

The possibilities are unlimited and they challenge and develop the trainer's creativity. The ultimate goal here can be to "make it worse", meaning that the stallion is trained in an environment that is saturated with more stimuli than he would probably ever be likely to encounter at an event. Thanks to this successive desensitisation, hardly anything will unsettle the stallion in later life.
However, please always make sure that the demands are built up step by step. Otherwise you run the risk of overwhelming the stallion. The result would then be the opposite of what you want to achieve: your stallion would become more afraid of the situation instead of becoming accustomed to it in the long term.

Problem management

Neither a stallion nor its owner is a perfectly predictable machine, so tricky and potentially dangerous situations can arise under unfavourable circumstances, not just when early education has been insufficient, but in spite of careful rearing and training. For this reason, we have drawn up emergency plans in the following section that aim to help you respond correctly in an emergency and to get the situation under control again as successfully as possible. These are first-aid measures, rather than training tips. It goes without saying that, once the situation has been resolved, you need to get to the bottom of what caused it and take measures to be able to better prevent something similar from happening in the future. What was considered to have been appropriate training may not have been good enough and specific training with an experienced trainer may be the solution. Or perhaps somebody was careless and did not shut a stable door properly, which should preferably never happen again.

The following applies to all of the situations described below: keep calm and prioritise the safety of the people involved.

Rearing, kicking, biting…

Stallions who rear behind the handler when being led, perhaps even striking out at their handler as they do so, have been given just as little clear training as stallions who kick out when being groomed, try to bite when being saddled or want to break away in the direction of other horses when being led. We believe that this is not a problem as such but a lack of basic education. If a stallion displays this kind of bad behaviour, consistent corrective training is absolutely essential. When thinking about corrective training, the issues described above should be considered and a professional trainer called upon if necessary. By taking these measures, the inadequate training can be caught up on, as a rule, and the stallion will become easy to control in everyday life. At this point, we should remember again that absolute consistency (not to be confused with violence!) is required when dealing with stallions. If you "turn a blind eye" every now and then, you will not have any long-term success and, in the worst case, you risk the horse becoming a danger to his environment.

The stallion mounts another horse

When being led across the yard, unloaded, groomed or even under saddle, a stallion may still pull away or otherwise break free, despite all precautions. In the worst case, there will be other horses around that the loose stallion will attempt to mount. This is a dangerous situation for all people and animals involved.

We cannot give across-the-board instructions because procedure depends greatly on the individual scenario and the conditions in which it takes place.

If you are quick enough and manage to safely grab the reins or rope, you can try to

This meeting was unplanned. People should not intervene in a situation like this under any circumstances, to avoid putting themselves at risk.

augurs less well and is no less dangerous. The stallion will either not even notice this attempt or will mount the other horse, which does not defuse the situation at all.

If the stallion you are riding mounts a riderless horse, you should try to dismount if possible and first get far enough out of the danger zone that you cannot be kicked by the horse that has been mounted. The measures described above can then be taken. If, to make matters worse, there is still a rider on the horse the stallion mounts, they should also try to dismount as quickly as possible. If the stallion has already mounted the other horse, the decision must be made as to whether dismounting is still possible and whether it is the less dangerous choice. Climbing down at the shoulder in front of the saddle is definitely an option in such situations. Of course, the best thing is not to wait this long, but to jump off in good time as a precaution if a loose stallion approaches.

Before everything spins out of control because of heavy-handed intervention and the danger for people and animals becomes even greater, there is also the option of creating a safe distance between you and the horses and simply waiting. The horse that the stallion is trying to mount will either defend itself by kicking and the stallion will dismount, or you will have to wait until mating is complete and catch the stallion then. If a mare in season is actually successfully covered during such an incident, unintended pregnancy can usually easily be prevented by a vet who will administer a douche or the appropriate medication. The owner of the stallion normally bears the costs of the procedure.

pull the stallion off. If you see the danger coming, you can try to grab the intended "victim" before the stallion mounts, turn it around and preferably take it to the safety of a stable. If there is a hose nearby, a well-aimed jet can help to regain the attention of a stallion that has already mounted another horse.

Bringing a more attractive "object" (a mare in season, for example) into view as a distraction

A serious fight between stallions is difficult to stop.
Serious injuries may result.
(Photo: Slawik)

When two aggressive stallions meet

It is possible to ride several stallions together in an arena or even in a field without any problems. Stallions will usually also stand peacefully next to one another when tied up in the grooming area. If they bump into each other with their hindquarters, they may kick out, but this is usually relatively easy to intercept.

Things become more difficult when two dominant stallions meet head-to-head. Whether they are loose, tied up or being led or ridden, this kind of situation can result in a serious scrap.

It usually begins with relatively harmless-seeming mutual sniffing, followed by squealing and attempts to bite each other on the head, neck or chest. The next step is stamping with the front feet and rearing.

If both stallions are being ridden, biting poses a great danger. The stallion could miss his opponent and bite the rider's limbs instead. In this case, only one option remains, namely you have to do everything you can to get rid of the attacker.

If the horses are loose or if you have not already nipped the beginnings in the bud and the situation has escalated, which often ends in torn ropes and loose horses, a show-down will begin that can involve considerable injury to the subordinate animal simply because of the usual lack of space and the resulting lack of opportunity for him to flee. Increased aggression in one of the stallions or in both animals due to lack of work can make this kind of fight particularly explosive.

Simply waiting until the opponents, who will often be rearing and sometimes "locking horns" with each other, stop is therefore not advisable. First of all, it is important to get all people present to safety and, if possible, to block off the area so that the stallions cannot run away and perhaps pose a hazard to road traffic. Now you will need strong helpers who are experienced with stallions. If one of the horses is still tied up, you must try to untie it and possibly lead it away immediately, thus ending the situation. You can try, for example, to drive loose, fighting horses forwards because, if they have to run, they cannot concentrate on fighting anymore and can kick out at the most. While one helper keeps the horses moving, others can try, if possible, to separate them. One option would be an improvised fence. In a field, you can also try to drive one stallion through the gate and quickly close it again in front of the nose of the other one.

Under no circumstances should the helpers throw themselves between the stallions or even form a human chain to separate them. This could prove fatal.

Highly aroused stallions

A highly aroused, prancing stallion with his tail held high may be a wonderful sight and, as long as he is displaying this behaviour in a well-fenced field or while loose in the arena, it is no problem. However, if a stallion gets so excited when being led that he becomes unresponsive, he poses a danger to the handler and, if the handler completely loses control, the stallion puts everything and everyone around him at risk. The same applies to the ridden stallion. It is normally not possible for the rider's aids to get them through a situation like this.

Regardless of whether the stallion is being led or ridden, it goes without saying that all of the people in the vicinity must be brought to safety first. If you are not already in an arena or other fenced area, the stallion must be guided into a safely enclosed environment (indoor school, yard, field or whatever is available at the time). As a rider, you will have to decide for yourself whether you are better staying on the horse's back or jumping off as soon as the opportunity presents itself. Now it is a question of waiting until the stallion has calmed down again.

The next thing to do is investigate where the sudden change in behaviour came from. For example, if, during the breeding season, a stallion is only brought out of his stable

Once a stallion becomes this excited, he is beyond human control. Now it is a question of waiting until he calms down again. (Photo: Slawik)

to cover a mare, he will soon become conditioned to becoming highly aroused as soon as he leaves his stable. A specific location on the site should always be designated for covering mares. If the stallion is allowed to mate with mares everywhere, sometimes in the stable corridor, sometimes in the indoor arena and sometimes in the field, strict control in the long term will be difficult. If the behaviour is attributable to one of these causes, the structure needs to be changed. Another possible cause could be a change in the immediate environment. For example, is there a new mare at the yard that is being exercised nearby? In that case this stimulus should be removed immediately. However, a situation such as this also shows that you should not just go back to business as usual but work on basic training. The same applies if you cannot find a genuine reason for the stallion's reaction. In this case, it is very likely to be a training problem that needs to be tackled straight away.

Grading of stallions

Internationally successful: the German Warmblood.
(Photo: Ostwald)

Stallion grading is a process where the stallion must meet various requirements and perform exercises. When all of the tests have been passed, the stallion is considered to be suitable for passing on his qualities and will be entered into the relevant studbook. Studbooks are maintained by a number of organisations – for instance, there is the Warmblood Breeders' Studbook, breed-specific studbooks such as the British Hanoverian Horse Society Studbook, and the Anglo European Studbook, for horses involved in competitions.

The question of why stallion grading is necessary in the first place is easy to answer. Without grading and the associated provisional entry into the respective studbook, the

offspring cannot be recorded in any of the books. This guarantees that only the best stallions of each breed influence its development. For many breeds, long-term entry in the studbook is also associated with a performance test.

Selection for **breeding purposes**

German Warmblood

Grading criteria for Warmblood breeds vary from one country to another and from one studbook to another, but probably the classic (and most quoted example) of how the grading system works in practice is that used by the Hanoverian Verband in Germany. The Hanoverian Verband has one of the most thorough, rigorous and demanding processes for grading of both mares and stallions of all studbooks. The success of Hanoverian Warmbloods worldwide at the very top of dressage and showjumping is a testimony to the breeding programme.

An understanding of the Hanoverian grading system is therefore vital for anyone considering breeding showjumpers or dressage horses anywhere in the world. Every aspect of the Hanoverian grading system is designed to fulfil the specified breeding aim of the Hanoverian Verband. In short, this is a horse with good rideability which, on the basis of its natural abilities, its temperament and character, is suitable as a performance horse as well as a pleasure horse.

On this basis, the federation strives for the breeding of talented sport horses in the disciplines of dressage, showjumping, eventing and driving.

The activities of the federation are all structured to ensure that of the 9,000 or more foals born every year that are eligible to be registered, only the very best are kept for breeding Hanoverian competition horses of the future. By the time a stallion is seven years old, he could be one of as few as twelve in his age group to be still approved for use at stud. The grading process itself is an extremely lengthy one, taking in as it does exhaustive assessment of conformation, paces, rideability and ability to pass on inherited talent.

Breeders may present their colts for what is known as an initial inspection by the relevant breed association at the age of two to two-and-a-half years. The requirements to be met are the same for all Warmbloods: the stallion must be registered for the breeding region in question and full papers must be brought along. The grading committee makes its first selection at the initial inspection. The colt is examined with regard to appearance and type: does the horse fit into the breed and the breeding aims of the association? Could it further the breed? Is the horse already big enough? Are there shortcomings such as weak basic paces or a poor topline? If there are considerable shortcomings, there may be doubts about the stallion's "durability". However, it is also possible for a stallion to have shortcomings but to make up for them with other positive attributes so that approval for grading may still be granted. In many cases, it is advisable to accept the verdict if the stallion does not satisfy

A Warmblood stallion being presented on tarmac.
(Photo: Ostwald)

the committee's requirements. If you are nevertheless still convinced of the stallion's qualities, you can try to present the horse to a different breed association. Grading through sport is also possible if the stallion later demonstrates exceptional potential in this area. However, the final decision is also taken by the relevant grading committee.

If the stallion matches the requirements profile of the relevant breed association at the initial inspection, he is permitted to attend the actual grading.

Gradings usually take place in autumn or winter. At gradings, characteristics such as type, conformation, basic paces, free jumping and balance are tested. The evaluation of these criteria is rather subjective and depends on the ideas and aims of each breed association. For example, a horse with essentially correct conformation may not score very highly because it does not match the breed association's current ideal.

The stallion should be suitably prepared for the grading. In addition to having been fed correctly and well cared for, this also includes ground work such as lungeing on single and double lunge reins, loose schooling and going for walks, because an impor-

Free jumping is part of grading for German Warmbloods and should be practised first. (Photo: Slawik)

tant criterion for grading is what is known as presentation of movement. The stallion should be given ample opportunity to develop his movement so that he shows himself off to his best advantage at the grading, where he is expected to maintain rhythm in all paces. At the walk, attention is paid to diligence and ground cover, at the trot to lightness, moment of suspension and hindquarter activity and, at the canter, to ground cover, an uphill tendency or possible overbalance.

Free jumping should also be practised in advance. It is important to note that dressage horses also have to take part in free jumping so that their physical awareness can be evaluated. Free jumping also demonstrates the horse's jumping ability, the size of the canter strides, jumping technique and carefulness. These criteria are also evaluated fairly subjectively.

The prepared horse will be examined by the grading committee over two to three days. Horses are usually shown on a tarmac surface or on a triangular track first, where the horse is shown in-hand and stands side-on in front of the judges on a hard concrete/paving surface so that his type and the quality of his conformation can be evaluated. The judges then evaluate the walk and trot in-hand. On the same day, the horses demonstrate their free movement in an indoor arena, to evaluate the trot and canter. Free jumping takes place on the second day. For free jumping, a lane that channels the horse down the middle, normally with three jumps, is set up. The jumps are smaller for dressage horses than they are for showjumpers. Regardless of which discipline they are intended for, free jumping is about how

well the horse solves the problem of jumping. The result of the grading is announced on the same day and may be either "graded", "not graded" or "temporarily not graded". Stallions that are temporarily not graded may be presented for grading again the following year. However, the older a stallion is, the more deductions there normally are. The upper age limit also varies here and is regulated by the association. All stallions that have actually been graded are now provisionally entered in Stallion Book I and authorised to breed actively with mares in the first season after grading. Depending on the guidelines of the association, they may only be allowed to cover a certain number of mares. However, grading alone is not enough to allow a stallion to cover mares for the rest of his life. Proof of performance is now required and there are several ways to achieve this.

The first way is the 30-day performance test, also known as the 30-day test. The 30-day test is mainly for three-year-old colts. Stallion performance tests often take place when stallions have already covered mares for a season. The test lasts for at least 30 days, during which the stallions may not leave the testing station. The purpose of this is to standardise the environmental influences for all horses so that their performance can be better compared. The stallions have the chance to get used to their environment and are less distracted. Each stallion is allocated a rider who trains him individually. Throughout the entire training phase, the horses are regularly examined and graded by the training committee to keep track of their development. At the final examination,

A four-year-old stallion in training, hopefully on the way to a dazzling career. (Photo: Ostwald)

the final examination committee evaluates the horse within the context of the exercises to be performed. As in the training phase, walk, trot, canter and aptitude for jumping are evaluated, both free and under saddle. The examination lasts for two days. On both days, the allocated test rider first presents the horse in its basic paces or rides a standardised exercise and then an unfamiliar rider tests and evaluates the horse's rideability. On the second day, ridden work is followed by free jumping.

If he passes the test, the stallion is temporarily registered in Stallion Book I again. There are basic tests for stallions to pass at four and five years old. Again, the results depend on the provisions of the breed associations. Instead of these basic or performance tests, it is also possible to qualify for

the federal championships, but this does not mean that the stallion has to take part or be placed in them. Qualification alone is sufficient. The performances delivered are graded with index points. Depending on the number of points gained, the stallion is entered into Stallion Book I or II, whereby stallions with higher numbers of points are entered into Stallion Book I. If a stallion does not achieve enough index points, he can also be ungraded, in which case he is not registered and is not given a breeding licence.

Once stallions have been registered successfully, they may usually mate with mares for life.

As well as this route, having the stallion complete the 70-day test at four years old, after the 30-day test, is also popular. The timeframe for the test is at least 70 days, during which time the horses do not leave the testing station. Again, each stallion is allocated a specific rider from the testing station who is responsible for day-to-day training and who must adapt themselves individually to the stallion. During the training phase, the training committee go to see the rider–stallion pair to check on their development. The 70-day test also includes cross-country suitability and showjumping, along with testing of the basic paces, rideability and free jumping. This is also compulsory for dressage stallions and the horses are even ridden by two different, unfamiliar riders. Again, the final examination takes place over two days. On the first day, the test rider presents the stallion's basic paces by riding a standardised exercise and then rideability is evaluated by an unfamiliar rider. Free jumping and cross-country are tested on the second day. The 70-day test can therefore be replaced by the 30-day test with subsequent performance tests. It is important to know that stallions that complete the 70-day test aged four years or older are only authorised to cover mares for the first season after grading and stallions that are just only three years old are authorised to cover mares for the first year after grading. They are only allowed to breed again afterwards when the 70-day test has been passed successfully. As things presently stand, the 70-day test can be bypassed if the stallion achieves a grading mark of 7.5 or higher in a class A dressage or showjumping test. As a five or six year old, he must qualify for the federal championships by achieving a grading mark of 8.0 or higher at selected competitions. Horses aged three or four years are nominated for the federal championships and qualification is then possible at five years old.

In addition to the route through grading, it is also still possible to qualify the stallion through proof of performance in sport. At the moment, five top-three placings in class S (dressage or showjumping) are required. This means that an older stallion that has been successful in sport can still be graded. To apply for grading, the horse owner must present proof of performance to the respective breed association, along with the application for grading. These cases are dealt with individually. Characteristics such as type and outward appearance are not simply ignored in cases of sporting success and sporting achievement can only result in permission to apply for grading. The grading committee will decide whether grading actually takes place during regular grading. However, horses that are successful in sport usually have such good conformation that they meet the requirements or, to put it another way, horses with poor conformation rarely enjoy above-average success in sport.

The Anglo European Studbook

The AES is a British-based studbook for performance horses, recognised by the Department for Environment, Food and Reval Affairs (Defra) and by the European Union (EU). It is a full member of the World Breeding Federation of Sports Horses, and maintains close links with the National Equine Database.

At present the AES has over 350 Approved stallions standing at stud in Britain and Europe, over 400 Licensed and over 150 Registered. The vast majority of the Approved stallions are at either grade A Showjumping, Advanced level Dressage or Eventing and almost half are, or have been, competing at the top International levels.

To become a graded stallion with the AES the stallion must undergo a stringent five-stage vetting first of all and show a great deal of talent for either dressage or showjumping at the initial stallion grading show, after which they must prove themselves in the sport during competitions. The selection is continuous and tough: stallions can be downgraded as well as being upgraded.

All these stallions are issued with certificates to prove their current status assuring breeders of using highly graded, sound, bona fide stallions with very good performance records.

Stallion shows are generally held in April and November each year, in Holland, France, Ireland and England. A preliminary of grading is a five-stage vetting. A good quality copy of a horse's pedigree is also assessed, together with any competition results.

The grading involves trotting up, in-hand, and loose jumping for two-and-a-half to three-year-old stallions, and trotting up followed by jumping under saddle for four-year-old stallions. Dressage stallions must perform a short dressage test.

If a stallion is graded, upon payment of a fee it will receive a grading certificate and covering certificates.

Stallions are graded at four different levels depending on age, ability, competition level, offspring production and offspring competition levels. Entry into a grading show does not automatically ensure that a stallion is graded even at a basic level.

Registered	Licensed	Approved	Approved Elite
This is the basic level of grading and normally young stallions attending their first grading would enter at this level if graded. Registered Grade stallions can cover up to 10 of their owner's mares per annum.	At this level a stallion should be competing in age classes and can cover up to 30 mares per annum.	This is the maximum level of grading and usually applies to stallions competing or that have competed at an International level, or that have proven offspring. Approved Grade stallions can cover an unlimited number of mares.	Stallions are given Elite status subject to the judges' discretion and based on proven competition and offspring success at the highest level.

Small, but powerful! German Riding Ponies look like miniature German Warmbloods and they are power-packed. (Photo: Slawik)

German Riding Pony

Grading of German Riding Ponies works in a similar way to Warmblood grading, but the grading procedure is different. As well as grading through sport, there are again two options for long-term registration in the stallion book. The first route is the 30-day test, which is intended for three- to six-year-old stallions. The performance test comes after the preliminary training test. In the performance test, temperament and basic paces are evaluated and aptitude for jumping is tested in free jumping and showjumping. There is also a cross-country test. The 30-day test for German Riding Ponies therefore corresponds to the 70-day test for Warmbloods. Ponies are entered into the stallion book once they have passed the 30-day test.

The second option consists of a short examination and subsequent federal championship qualification. The short test lasts for two days. Free jumping takes place on the first day. In addition, the pony also completes a dressage test under its own, as well as under an unfamiliar, rider. On the second day, a level A showjumping course must be ridden, after which rideability is tested again by an unfamiliar rider. The pony stallion is ridden by adult riders during this short test. In order to qualify for the federal championships as a five or six year old, the pony must be successfully presented at competitions by a child or teenager. Qualification is possible in the disciplines of jumping, dressage or eventing. In the course of a year, two competitions per federal state are advertised for the purpose of qualification. People may take part in them regardless of which federal association they belong to. Qualification alone is sufficient for German Riding Ponies too, and participation in the federal championships or even placing is not necessary.

Hardy Icelandic horses are late developers and are normally presented for grading at three years old, at the earliest.

Icelandic horses

Icelandic horses tend to be late developers, so most stallions are presented at grading events as three year olds at the youngest. To be allowed to attend a grading event, stallions must have successfully completed a young horse examination no longer than twelve months ago. Stallions are presented in-hand and loose during grading. Specially trained judges from the grading committee evaluate the gait potential of the young stallions, along with their external appearance. The most important thing here is that the young stallion shows a natural tendency to tölt. The grading committee's result is announced at the end of the event. The graded stallion may now actively breed with mares during the first season. Icelandic stallions are usually broken to ride at four to four-and-a-half years. The material examination usually takes place when the stallion is five years old and is a five gait test where the stallion is shown under saddle on an oval track, in all five gaits: walk, trot, canter, tölt and flying pace. Tölt is compulsory in all cases, but flying pace is not. If flying pace is not shown, the horse will receive a poor mark, but this mark can be compensated for by the evaluation of the other gaits.

There are relatively few Icelandic horses, so their gradings take place together with gradings for other breeds. Icelandic horses are only recognised as such if they are either pure bred or all of their ancestors can be traced back to ancestors exclusively born in Iceland.

Purebred Arabians

In order for a purebred Arabian stallion to be graded, he must have a pedigree certificate that proves that his lineage can be traced back without any gaps and that his ancestors are recognised purebred Arabians only. Blood typing or DNA analysis with parentage testing for the stallion is also required. Breeding of purebred Arabians is pure, which means that other breeds may not be involved.

For Arabian stallions, presentation for grading is possible at three years old at the youngest. During grading, the external appearance, basic paces and free jumping ability of the unshod stallion are evaluated. Successfully graded Arabians must complete a stallion performance test in order to be entered into the stallion book in the long term. There are a variety of different options for this. What is known as the station test lasts for at least 70 days and consists of a preliminary training test and a performance test. A cross-country test is also taken, in addition to evaluation of rideability, temperament, gaits and jumping ability. Other options that deliver the performance necessary for registration are field tests in various disciplines. Depending on predisposition and breeding purpose, the stallion can compete as a driving horse, in a cross-country test, condition test, in Western riding, in a rideability test or in a distance test. The performance test can also be taken by means of a specific number of placings at competitions. Last but not least, a performance test through racing is also possible for purebred Arabians. For long-term registration in the stallion book, success specified by the

Arabians have been pure bred for centuries.
(Photo: Slawik)

competent authority must have been achieved in flat racing.

English Thoroughbred

Unlike Warmbloods, English Thoroughbreds are not graded. Instead, studbooks are used to establish suitability for breeding. In Britain, the importance of horseracing is reflected in the impressive longevity of the General Stud Book, first published in 1793. This was the original breed registry of British horses and was used to document the breeding of Thoroughbreds and related foundation bloodstock such as the Arabian horse.

Britain is home to over 5,000 Thoroughbred breeders. From commercial enterprises to small "hobby" breeders, stud farms are located the length and breadth of Britain. Although modern life has affected parts of the countryside, Britain lends itself to lush pastures and its temperate climate makes for ideal breeding conditions.

Long legs, elegant conformation and clearly defined musculature characterise the English Thoroughbred. (Photo: Slawik)

The Thoroughbred Breeders' Association, which has over 2,000 members, is the only official body representing Thoroughbred breeders in Great Britain. It has around 350 registered stallions, and over 10,000 brood-mares, which produce a total approaching 6,000 foals each year. There are more than 2,200 commercial stud farms.

It must be possible to prove that stallions can be traced back to a stallion and a mare that were both registered in a studbook before 1980 (also called a "strain"). Furthermore, it must be possible to trace the ancestors of the stallion in question in at least eight consecutive generations and these eight generations must originate from the afore-mentioned strain. It is therefore not enough to be able to trace the sire and dam of the stallion back to the horses registered before 1980. There must also not any horses in the stallion's lineage in the eight interim generations that cannot be traced back to these studbooks.

A rider in traditional dress on a Portuguese Lusitano with traditional tack. (Photo: Ostwald)

Baroque horses

Lusitanos are graded all over the world under the same conditions by the grading committee of the APSL (Associação Portuguesa de Criadores do Cavalo Puro Sangue Lusitano). It sets high requirements for Lusitano stallions and their owners. Only horses both of whose parents have been graded by the APSL and therefore have valid breeding papers are permitted to be graded and can be entered into the adult register (Livro de Adultos) of the stallion book, following successful evaluation by the grading committee of the APSL. At grading, stallions aged four at the youngest and ten at the oldest are initially presented to the competent panel of judges, under saddle, in some kind of division into the three basic paces. Following successful collective evaluation, the judges call up each stallion again individually to evaluate its basic paces and rideability. The sequence of this presentation is determined by the panel of judges, so the exercise for one stallion may differ from that for another. Afterwards, the stallions are unsaddled at the edge of the arena and presented to the judges again. The results are then announced publicly.

A breeding stallion that has proven himself through his own achievements may be classed as a Reproductor Recomendado (recommended stud stallion) and a breeding stallion whose offspring have been subject to a quality test can be identified as Reproductor de Merito (excellent stud stallion). At the basic grading, Pura Raza Española (PRE; Spanish Purebred) stallions of at least three years old are only presented in-hand or on the lunge in the basic paces. Initially, they are not evaluated under saddle. The judging panel is put together by ANCCE (Associacion Nacional de Criadores de Caballos Pura Raza Española). It is advisable for stallion owners not to present their stallions to judges as three year olds. Iberian horses are usually late developers, so they may not have reached the minimum height required for grading at this age or there may be growth-related conformational flaws that would result in a poor evaluation. PRE stallions that have been presented to the grading committee but not graded will never be allowed into the stallion book.

Stallions may later qualify for Reproductor Calificado and Reproductor de Élite based on their own achievements. At the Calificado grading, the stallion's external appearance is initially very closely examined and evaluated. Only stallions that correspond to the breeding objective in every detail, right down to the shape of the nostrils, have a chance of recognition as Calificado sires. Evaluation under saddle in the basic paces then follows. This must also be exceptional in every respect. Finally, the stallion is examined for any hereditary diseases. For this purpose, sperm samples are taken, DNA tests are carried out and X-rays are taken of the limbs. Following successful Calificado grading, shipping of semen is also permitted, which is still forbidden among stallions with only basic grading. In a manner of speaking, Élite grading is an extended Calificado grading. Performance of offspring is included in the evaluation here. Sperm from an Élite stallion may also be shipped. Until now, both gradings have only taken place in

These Dutch carriage horses are now popular all over Europe as show and leisure horses. (Photo: Slawik)

Spain and only basic grading by the grading committee of the ANCCE is common across Germany. However, the German breed association is trying to make Calificado grading possible in Germany too.

Grading of Lipizzaners works in a similar way to grading of PREs. Stallions must be four years old and over, when they are shown in-hand in the basic paces, in front of the judging panel. Judges may also request presentation under saddle and in harness. Unlike PREs, Lipizzaners that are not successful at their first grading may be presented at a subsequent grading. However, this is only the case if they were not older than six at the first grading.

In the case of Friesians, stallion owners have the option of presenting their stallion to the public at various FPZV (Friesian Horse Breed Association) breed shows first. If the stallion makes a positive impression at these shows with regard to conformation and movement, it makes sense to present him for grading the next year. However, stallions may also be presented to the grading committee without this advance evaluation. At the grading, the horse is evaluated in its basic paces, loose and in-hand, as well as stood and measured in front of the judges. If stallions have already completed their fifth year of life when presented for grading, they may only finally be permitted to breed after successful completion of a 50-day test.

The KFPS (Koninlijke Friesch Paarden Stamboek) also has other, very strict selection criteria that must be fulfilled before grading. For example, when Friesian stallions aged at least two and a half years are registered, they are subject to X-ray examinations of their limbs to avoid hereditary diseases. These X-rays are compulsory for every horse and must be produced at entry into Stallion Book I at the latest. In order to save the owner unnecessary costs, the breed association recommends having stallions examined before registering for grading. This way, it will soon become apparent whether there is actually any chance of eventual registration in the stallion book. A DNA test that not only provides evidence of the pure breeding of the stallion over at least four generations, but also the absence of the red factor (chestnut gene), must be available by registration at the latest. In doing so, the gene, which may result in offspring of the unwanted chestnut colour if two carriers mate, can be completely eliminated from breeding.

Quarter Horses

Grading of Western horses works in a similar way to grading of Warmblood sports horses. Stallions may be presented to the grading committee aged 24 months at the youngest and must satisfy the requirements of the German Quarter Horse Association. Proof of pedigree, height and cannon bone and chest circumference are tested. The stallion is also tested on a paved surface. Afterwards, the stallion is presented on a triangular track in walk and trot and then all three basic paces must be shown on the lunge. There are five individual grades in total, which must result in an overall grade of 7.0 or higher for the stallion to be considered to have been graded.

Following grading, it is compulsory for Quarter Horses to complete a stallion performance test. The necessary achievements must be accomplished in reining, trail, pleasure and Western riding exercises. Again, from the 20 sub-components of the stallion performance test, a certain overall grade, which is assigned by the breeding board and the selected judges, has to be achieved.

Terminology

The male parent of a horse, a stallion, is commonly known as the sire and the female parent, the mare, is called the dam. Both are important in the genetic make-up of the ensuing offspring

Foundation bloodstock or foundation stock are horses that are the progenitors, or foundation, of a new horse breed or a given bloodline within a breed.

Foundation sire: a particularly outstanding stallion with above-average talent, identified as the original progenitor of the breed. A foundation mare is the corresponding female. In many cases, foundation mares are not always identified in old pedigree records.

Studbook: a breed registry, or official list of horses within a specific breed whose parents are known.

A closed studbook does not accept any outside blood. The registered animals and all subsequent offspring trace back to the foundation stock. This ensures that the animal is a purebred member of the breed. An example of a closed studbook is that of the Thoroughbred, with a studbook tracing back to 1791.

An open studbook usually has strict studbook selection criteria that require an animal to meet a certain standard of conformation, performance or both. This allows breeders to modify breeds by including individuals who conform to the breed standard but are of outside origin. Some horse breeds allow crossbreds who meet specific criteria to be registered. One example is the semi-open studbook of the American Quarter Horse, which still accepts horses of Thoroughbred breeding.

Another form of open registry is a registry based on performance or conformation, called in some societies registry on merit (ROM). In such registries, an eligible animal that meets certain criteria is eligible to be registered on merit, regardless of ancestry. In some cases, even unknown or undocumented ancestry may be permitted.

The Quarter Horse is the epitome of the Western horse.
(Photo: Ostwald)

Mare and stallion look pleasant at first glance, but that alone is not enough for breeding high-performance offspring. (Photo: Ostwald)

Ungraded stallions as sires

Owners of stallions, but also of mares, often wish at least once for their own horse to produce offspring. This is entirely understandable, but you should give serious thought to whether making this wish come true is sensible, for the good of the horse. We want to look at everything from the point of view of the stallion owner who is either interested in their stallion producing a foal for themselves or who has been approached by a mare owner about whether their stallion would be available to sire a foal from their mare.

You should be aware that a stallion is far from being a good sire just because he is very easy to handle, a wonderful partner for leisure or sport or simply because he is your own beloved horse. There is usually a reason why a stallion has not been graded or was not even presented for grading in the first place. Knowingly allowing external or other defects to be passed on is irresponsible. Breeding partners should be chosen carefully and should not simply be "the stallion (or mare) next door". You should also remember that the act of mating always presents a risk. Injuries, possibly caused by the mare kicking out, are not uncommon and you should not expose your stallion to this risk "just for fun".

If not just you but other, independent horse experts recognise that the stallion has qualities that would make him a good sire and grading has just not been attempted until now for whatever reason, you should still try to go down this official route. It is a worthwhile step from a breeding point of view because if only the mare is registered and not the stallion, the foal will only get half a paper, which will reduce its value at sale.

An ungraded stallion may also produce offspring without anyone intending him to do so. This may be because he broke out and had access to a mare in season, because nobody knew he was a cryptorchid (one testicle is concealed in the abdomen) and he was allowed to run with mares because people assumed he was a gelding or because he was raised in a mixed herd and not separated from the mares early enough.

But what are the consequences of unsuitable or even unwanted mating? In the best case, the stallion (as well as the mare) actually has potential and a healthy, perhaps even very talented foal is born. In this case, the only shortcoming could be that the foal would not have any papers and its owners would only be able to sell it for a lower price as a result. However, if one or both

All foals are cute, but health and good conformation are much more important. (Photo: Ostwald)

parents were not suitable for breeding, mild to severe external defects or health impairments in the foal may be possible or even probable. It is the same with foals that result from unintended incest. In this case, crippled or non-viable foals may even be born. Every stallion owner should be aware of these scenarios and behave with the appropriate level of responsibility.

Breeding **practice**

Nowadays, there are three main practices in horse breeding, namely hybridisation, pure breeding and refinement.

In the case of hybridisation, which was used in the twentieth century and earlier, available horses were mated together haphazardly. It therefore cannot be considered

Purebred and still pure today: the Icelandic horse, shown here at the tölt, the gait typical of the breed. (Photo: Slawik)

to be a systematic breeding method, but was just about "production" of offspring. If possible, different breeds were mated together to avoid incest. Today, the following practices are common.

In cross-breeding, we attempt to combine the features of two (or more) existing breeds. This could be described as a kind of intentional hybridisation, but one that is always supported by the blood of horses from the original breed. It is therefore not random, but follows a specific purpose, namely creation of a new breed.

In pure breeding practices, only horses of the same breed are mated together. In this practice, we talk about "closed studbooks". Most purebred animals are very similar both with regard to their appearance and their characteristics. The breed associations keep studbooks. Examples of pure breeds are the Arabian, the English Thoroughbred and the Icelandic horse. Pure breeding requires a high degree of logistical expenditure, because horses must be travelled over large distances at great expense in order to introduce "new blood" into existing hereditary lines within a breed. Shipping of deep frozen sperm and artificial insemination are useful here.

In the practice of refinement, the essential features of a breed are retained and are only expanded upon by a few desirable traits of horses of other breeds. English Thoroughbreds and Arabians are often used for refinement. In refinement, your own horse's qualities and those of the other horses available for pure breeding must constantly be observed to enable each breed's best qualities, such as particularly good move-

ment or jumping ability, to be recognised or used. Today, these two breeding practices (pure breeding and refinement) are the most important, especially in professional sport horse breeding, and are suitable for producing world-class horses. Because of the vast outlay in terms of administration, logistics and cost, they can often only be carried out consistently in very large studs.

Pure breeding and refinement are also the most interesting practices for private stallion owners. Breeders who own a stallion are usually connected to large, professional operations or make their stallions available at insemination centres. "Everyday" breeders, on the other hand, usually have one or more mares that they either take to the stallion or have artificially inseminated by a veterinarian at their own yard.

A digression into the genetics of **colour**

What dressage horse breeder wouldn't want one or, even better, several jet-black Totilas from their own mare? What breeder of Iberian horses wouldn't love to breed animals with unusual colours such as cremello and with a walk that would score a ten in classical dressage too? And who, as a stallion owner, wouldn't consider themselves lucky if they owned just the coveted sire that can make these wishes come true.

Unfortunately, science has not yet been able to find out how and on which alleles quality of pace is inherited. However,

*This would be the perfect sire for anybody
who wants a black horse. (Photo: Ostwald)*

colour has been researched to the greatest possible extent, barring a few exceptions, and we would like to briefly present the findings here.

The basic terminology

The outer appearance of a horse (phenotype) is determined by its genes (genotype). Each of these genes consists of two individual parts (alleles), one of which comes from the egg cell of the mother and the other from the semen of the father. The amalgamation of these two alleles results in a new combination of genes. The genotype of the resulting foal is therefore a mix of the genotypes of the parents.

Some genes prevail over others in the phenotype. These genes are described as being dominant (they are written in capital letters). The subordinate genes are described as recessive (they are written in small letters). If both alleles of a horse have the same characteristic (for example: dominant XX or recessive xx), they are called homozygous. Genotypes that are composed of a dominant and a recessive allele are heterozygous (for example: Xx).

Co-dominance, where both alleles of a heterozygous gene have the same value, is rarer. To make things clearer, let's take a brief trip into the world of flowers. In co-dominance, if you cross a white flower with a red flower, the alleles will not only mix in the genotype, but also in the phenotype. The flowers from this pairing will therefore be pink. In horses, we can see this in the "cream gene" that is neither covered by the basic colour nor covers the basic colour itself, but lightens it (for example a chestnut horse becomes a palomino or a cremello or brown becomes dun or perlino).

A lethal factor is a homozygous dominant gene (WW) with which the embryo or, in some cases, the neonate, is not viable and dies in the womb or shortly after birth.

Perlinos are quite a rare sight. (Photo: Ostwald)

The factors (genes)

The horse's colour therefore results from certain genes that are called factors. Genetically, horses only come in two basic colours: red and black. These two colours are diluted, covered up, combined, complemented with white or made into patterns by other genes, as the following table shows in an overview.

The factor	Dominant homozygous	Recessive homozygous	Heterozygous
A factor (agouti)	AA = brown	aa = black	Aa = brown
E factor (extension)	EE = black or brown	ee = chestnut	Ee= black or brown
G factor (grey)	GG = grey	gg = no grey	Gg = grey
D factor (dun)	DD = dun	dd = no dun	Dd = dun
Z factor (silver) no effect on chestnut	ZZ = black and brown are lightened (e.g. silver-grey)	zz = normal colour	Zz = black and brown are lightened (e.g. silver-grey)
F factor (flaxen)	FF = normal coloured long hair	ff = lightened long hair	Ff = normal coloured long hair
W factor (white)	WW = lethal factor	ww = normal colour	Ww = foal born white
Ch factor (champagne)	ChCh = champagne lightening	chch = normal colour	Chch = champagne lightening
Pa factor (pangare)	PaPa = lightening at the muzzle, eyes and flanks	papa = no effect	Papa = lightening at the muzzle, eyes and flanks

Sty factor (sooty)	StySty = darker base colour	stysty = normal base colour	Stysty = darker base colour
To factor (tobiano)	ToTo = tobiano	toto = solid-coloured	Toto = tobiano
Ov factor (overo)	OvOv = lethal factor	ovov = no overo pattern	Ovov = overo
Spl factor (splashed white)	SplSpl = splashed-white markings	splspl = solid-coloured	Splspl = splashed-white carrier
Rn factor (roan)	RnRn = roan	rnrn = solid-coloured	Rnrn = roan
Lp factor (appaloosa)	LpLp = appaloosa	lplp = solid-coloured	Lplp = appaloosa
P factor (pearl)	PP = no pearl features	pp = pearl	Pp = pearl features scarcely visible

The cr factor (the cream gene) cannot be listed in this table because it is co-dominant. If a horse carries this gene, lightening of the coat will result in all cases. If this gene is inherited from both parents (PcrPcr), lightening of the coat will be intense. If the gene is only inherited from one parent, lightening will be less pronounced.

The Spl factor (the splashed white gene) will show a phenotype with blue eyes, white belly, white legs, white face and white croup with a white tail in a homozygous dominant

In this stallion, the brindle stripes can be seen most clearly on the sides of the abdomen. (Photo: Ostwald)

genotype, while a heterozygous genotype will produce a phenotype with white markings on the head and legs and sometimes blue eyes; these horses are called splashed white carriers.

The Rn factor (the roan gene) leads to intermingling of white hairs. The amount of white hair varies from horse to horse and does not change over the course of life.

The P factor (the pearl gene) lightens the coat, as well as the mane and tail. Chestnuts become sandy coloured and black horses pale grey.

There are also other factors that cause dorsal stripes, stripes (known as "brindled" in dogs) or the different patterns in Appaloosas, for example. In the case of these factors, however, science has not yet been able to explain how they are inherited.

Basic colour genetics

In this tableau, we show how agouti and extension factors can influence the choice of breeding animals. The agouti and extension factors are responsible for the formation of the three basic phenotypical colours, black, brown and chestnut. Here we show which effects on colour the pairing of different parents can have.

Phenotype	Genotype	Possible offspring
Chestnut	aa; ee	Only black offspring will result if mated with a black horse, otherwise all colours
Chestnut	Aa; ee	All colours may result
Chestnut	AA; ee	No black offspring
Brown	AA; EE	Brown offspring only
Brown	AA; Ee	No black offspring
Brown	Aa; Ee	Can produce all colours
Brown	Aa; EE	Cannot produce chestnut

Rappe	aa; EE	Cannot produce chestnut and can only produce black if paired with a black horse
Rappe	aa; Ee	When paired with a black horse can only produce black, otherwise all colours

As shown in the table, the other factors are also inherited in this way (see first table) and therefore still influence the phenotype, in addition to the agouti and extension factors.

By observing the breeding animals they are interested in very closely, breeders have the chance almost to reliably determine the genotype, in the basic colours at least. Enough offspring must be available and the colour of the breeding partner must be known. For breeders who would like a black horse, for example, the foal of a black horse and a black horse will always be black, providing that the phenotype is not influenced by another factor, for example the silver gene.

and must meet a few requirements (see box). If these requirements are met, mating between the stallion and the mare may take place in different ways.

The minimum requirements for the stallion's fresh sperm are as follows: each ejaculation must produce at least 40 millilitres of semen, containing 100 million sperm per millilitre. The total semen sample must contain at least five billion sperm, 70 percent of which must be unimpaired. The semen must have a milky consistency and be milky white to blueish-grey in colour.

Types of **covering** and insemination

At the start of every breeding career, the sperm of the stallion must be investigated

The most natural form of covering is the natural mating that takes place in herds in the wild. For the purposes of breeding, natural mating can take place loose, which means that both the stallion and the mare can move freely in an area (often a smaller,

*Everything has gone smoothly with this natural mating.
Everybody involved is calm and the mare is not defending
herself. (Photo: Slawik)*

fenced-in area) without being held or tied up and the stallion can cover the mare without any outside influence. It is also possible for the mare to be tied up or held with a headcollar and rope. The stallion is then led to the mare and also held during mating. In these cases, both genders have direct contact with one another and the stallion can smell the mare in season.

Artificial insemination of mares is now very common. For artificial insemination, the stallion's semen has to be collected first. To collect the semen, the stallion is taken either to a real mare or to a dummy mare that mimics the size and physique of a real mare. To get the stallion to mount the dummy, an in-season mare, protected by a low wall, stands in front of the dummy to begin with, so that the stallion becomes aroused and mounts the dummy. With time and as a result of conditioning, the stallion will become aroused as soon as he sees the dummy and will usually mount it without any problems and then ejaculate, following his instincts. The semen is then collected by a person using a special container, known as an artificial vagina, and can now be used in different ways.

The artificial vagina is a tube-shaped device, usually made from plastic, into which the stallion's erect penis is inserted as soon as the stallion has mounted the dummy or a real mare. Real mares are used, for example, if the stallion is not sufficiently excited by a dummy.

It is now also possible to collect semen from the stallion while he is standing, without him having to mount a dummy. This avoids the injuries that can occur when mounting and dismounting from the dummy. It is beneficial for older stallions who suffer from joint or back problems, for example.

A certain temperature and certain pressure ratios must prevail in the artificial vagina so that it is similar to a real mare's vagina and causes the stallion to ejaculate. The exact parameters vary from stallion to stallion. Individual fine tuning of the artificial vagina to the stallion in question can even influence quantity and quality of sperm. The ideal temperature is normally between 38 and 42 degrees Celsius. After use, the artificial vagina should be cleaned with boiling water only, because residue from disinfectants or other chemicals could kill sperm at the next ejaculation.

The advantages of mounting a dummy mare are that semen can be collected from the stallion more frequently and that

The stallion is used to mounting the dummy mare. He bites onto the dummy as if it were a real mare, while semen is collected using an artificial vagina. (Photo: Slawik)

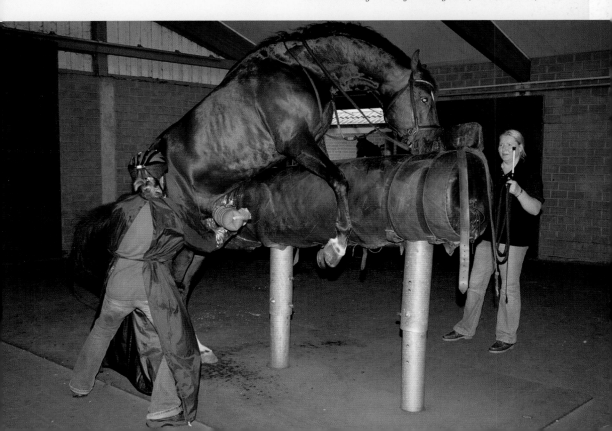

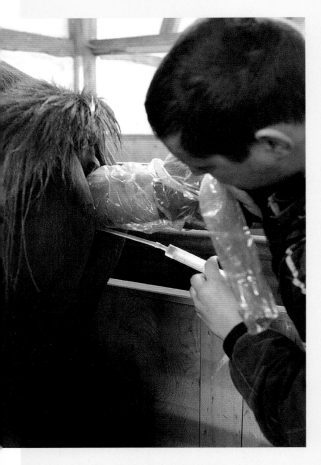

A mare being artificially inseminated: the sperm sample is in the syringe at the end of the long tube.
(Photo: Slawik)

The sperm collected can be used for insemination as soon as it has been divided into portions and prepared. The mare will preferably be on site and ready for mating. This can be determined by a vet using a "follicle test". The optimum period for insemination is from twelve hours before to twelve hours after ovulation. For the actual insemination, the sperm is inserted directly into the mare's womb using a long semen tube.

The samples of sperm can also be deep-frozen in a special procedure to make them long-lasting, meaning that a stallion can still produce offspring even after his death. The major advantage of deep-frozen over fresh sperm is that the individual sperm samples can be shipped. Another advantage of deep-frozen sperm is that semen does not have to be collected from sport stallions during the competition season but this can be postponed until a break in the season. However, the results of insemination with deep-frozen sperm are not as good as with fresh sperm, which is why breeders prefer the latter.

The decision about which stallion may mate with which mare is also not always left up to the owners. If you want to cross two different breeds, the relevant breed associations will specify the guidelines relevant for this, so you should find out about these guidelines first. For example, an Oldenburg stallion may, in principle, not just be authorised for Oldenburg, but perhaps also for Berlin-Brandenburg, so the stallion would therefore be permitted to mate with mares registered in Berlin-Brandenburg too. On the other hand, a Holsteiner stallion graded with the breed association for German

mating requires less energy and is less dangerous than mounting a real mare that may defend herself and, in the worst case, injure the stallion. A single sample of semen collected in the artificial vagina can be divided up into eight to twelve smaller samples that are enough to successfully inseminate mares. This means that the stallion can produce considerably more offspring than he could by natural mating.

horses is not necessarily permitted to mate with Holsteiner mares. For this authorisation, he would also have to be recognised by the Holsteiner breed association. Mares may also be entered into the studbook of several associations. If a mare has a foal sired by a stallion that was not authorised to cover her, this foal will not be given any papers or a brand. In normal cases, it is still possible to have the foal registered in the respective studbook, in consultation with the association with which the mare is registered and usually in return for payment.

Natural mating		Artificial insemination	
Pros	*Cons*	*Pros*	*Cons*
Mares are more stimulated so they can absorb semen more easily. Sperm cannot be mixed up. Mares that do not become pregnant easily can be successfully inseminated in this way.	Transmission of disease as a result of sperm that has not been cleaned first or because of inadequate hygiene. Risk of injury. Fewer fertilisations possible than with artificial insemination.	Full use can be made of sperm reserves, less strain for the stallion, possible to use the stallion in sport at the same time. Quality of the sperm stays the same. A sperm bank can be set up as a gene reserve. Protection against transmission of diseases, for example venereal diseases. Sperm can be shipped over vast geographical distances. Reduced risk of injury.	Collection of semen results in disproportionately high use of individual breeding stallions. Collection of semen, semen preparation and artificial insemination are usually only possible for financially well-placed operations. There are additional costs for the breeder because it involves costly and time-consuming processes. Private owners can take their stallions to this kind of establishment.

Species-appropriate stallion keeping

(Sports) stallions also have the right to turn-out and the chance of freedom. (Photo: Ostwald)

In order to be able to keep a stallion in a species appropriate way, we first need to be aware of his needs and the responsibilities that these needs entail for us. It is actually quite simple: stallions are horses, just like geldings and mares, so they have the same needs. They need contact with other members of their species, constant access to water and ideally also roughage, together with as much exercise as possible in a field or at least a paddock. Horses with a high drive for movement should also be trained and worked at least once a day. It is not the stallion's fault that these conditions are not as easy to create for him as they are for mares or geldings, because of his high sex drive. He cannot

do anything about his behaviour and the "hassle" that it causes for us humans. It is up to us to provide the stallion with a suitable environment and to ensure that he can easily find his way in it, through appropriate socialisation and training.

The better a stallion is socialised and reared and the more species appropriate his management, the easier he will be to handle, whether it is in everyday life, when covering mares or at public events.

We have already looked in detail at socialisation through species-appropriate rearing and training. In the following, we present different types of management and explain how these can be made as species-appropriate as possible, from a hatch in the stable that allows contact with the neighbour.

A stable with an adjoining paddock provides the stallion with variety when he isn't currently out in the field. (Photo: Ostwald)

We have been able to observe for years that keeping a stallion with geldings can work as well. In our herd, an old and a young stallion live with 25 geldings. This is the ideal scenario, because the stallions have freedom of movement and the company of other horses all day long. As a result, they are contented and well balanced. In this case, the stallion does not entail any extra effort for the owner or trainer in terms of managing exercise.

Some **basic information** first

If a horse is kept in a stable, it should not be smaller than a minimum size of (2.3 × height of the stallion's withers in metres)^2, on animal welfare grounds, and bigger is obviously better. Ideally, the stable will have a directly adjoining and freely accessible small paddock measuring at least 15 m^2. This allows even stabled stallions to walk at least a few strides straight at any time, which is a major benefit both for the mind and for keeping the horse's musculoskeletal system healthy. However, this small paddock under no circumstances replaces additional turn-out, at least four to five hours of which should be guaranteed every day. In principle, the following applies: the more turn-out a day, the more balanced the horse. Lack of turn-out often manifests itself in aggressive behaviour, especially where stallions are concerned.

The most species-appropriate types of management, i.e. an open barn with indoor and outdoor areas where horses have free access to pasture or a similar system where horses have to walk to different areas to access food and water etc., is unfortunately possible for only a few stallions. For a shared open barn with, for example, five horses, we recommend a minimum area of around 600 m^2 in order to avoid confrontations, fighting and scrapping. Horses have to be able to get out of each other's way and to maintain the necessary individual distance from each other. Very narrow fenced areas and those with lots of corners should also be avoided, because a low-ranking animal would not be able to flee safely and could easily be driven into a corner.

The stallion at **livery**

Keeping a stallion at a livery yard is often a challenge. The challenge begins with looking for a yard because stallions are far from welcome everywhere. If stallions are accepted, it is often only possible to keep them in a stable. Daily turn-out should definitely be guaranteed here, at the very least with visual contact with other horses, but preferably in the same field as a gelding or a herd of geldings. However, direct contact with other horses is only possible with an appropriately well socialised stallion, because he must not pose a threat to his field companions. As a responsible stallion owner, you should steer clear of a yard where stallions are allowed out for a short time at most and even then only when all of the other horses are back in their stable.

Livery yards should also allow stallions to be turned out with another horse, such as a gelding, for example. (Photo: Ostwald)

The location of the stable is important. If a barred "prison cell", well away from all the hustle and bustle and possibly out of sight and earshot of other horses, is the only accommodation intended for stallions, this yard is not the right choice. Sooner or later, being kept in isolation will lead to behavioural problems in horses of either gender. The stallion should be accommodated with other horses, preferably in a stable with a window where he can be involved in the everyday comings and goings. However, you should make sure that geldings, or other stallions, but not mares, are kept in the stables right next door. This is not always easy at yards where the horses change frequently.

Another factor not to be underestimated is the structure of the stallion's everyday life at the yard. On the one hand, this requires the owner to train his or her stallion well enough that he poses a risk neither to the staff when mucking out, feeding, leading out to grass and any other activities nor to the other liveries. It also means that you must be able to groom your stallion in a communal area in the presence of mares or to exercise him in the indoor or outdoor arena. On the other hand, you are also dependent on the understanding of the other liveries. Enjoyment of the hobby is quickly lost when over-cautious or spiteful mare owners make riding in the arena virtually impossible for you or even intentionally walk or ride provocatively close past your stallion.

Only if all of these factors are taken into account when choosing a yard are species-appropriate management for the stallion and a pleasant environment for his owner guaranteed.

The stallion at a **training yard**

The atmosphere and the structures at a training yard are clearly different from those at a normal livery yard. At a training yard, horses are not normally looked after and ridden by their owner, but are cared for by staff and trained and taken to competitions by riders. Here, the stallion owner is obliged to check carefully in advance whether everybody who

Competition horses in particular, from whom a high level of performance is required, need species-appropriate management with light, air, contact with other horses and preferably unlimited access to roughage. (Photo: Ostwald)

will deal with the horse can actually demonstrate adequate experience with stallions. It should be a given that species-appropriate management is maintained with all training. You should also definitely keep an eye on feeding practices. Performance horses need a lot more concentrate feed, as well as a different feed composition, from leisure horses, because they use up a lot of energy through training and the stress of competitions. This is usually taken into consideration at training yards. However, it is unfortunately often forgotten that sufficient roughage must also be available, preferably ad lib hay. Shocking figures show that around 55 percent of competition horses and up to 74 percent of racehorses suffer from stomach ulcers that can be attributed to stress combined with insufficient roughage.

If the horse is also going to be used for breeding, you should make sure that the staff have enough experience in this area and that they carry out the necessary hygiene measures, such as regular cleaning of the genitals. The fact that covering mares uses up a lot of energy that needs to be compensated for must also be taken into consideration in feeding.

Are stallions particularly "poor doers"?

We do often hear that stallions need more food than geldings or mares, but in general it isn't the case. The necessary feeding ration does not depend on gender, but on the individual physical and mental constitution of the horse and the work he or she does each day. Like any sports horse, a stallion used for competition has high energy requirements. Covering mares also uses particularly high amounts of energy, which needs to be taken into consideration when feeding. However, it is also about feeding the right amount. A stallion that covers 15 mares a week will certainly need a lot more extra energy than a stallion that only covers 30 mares throughout the entire season. The more mating he does, the more protein the stallion will need. But be careful: obesity or an excess of protein can impair breeding performance!

Along with appropriate feeding of concentrates, vitamin and mineral supplements should also be fed according to need in order to prevent deficiency symptoms or a steep decline in ability to perform.

The most beautiful stable is worth nothing if there is no contact with other horses. (Photo: Ostwald)

The stallion at **home**

If you keep your stallion privately in your own little yard, you will certainly have fewer problems, but you will also be responsible for making the environment species-appropriate yourself. This means that, along with adequate provision for space, feeding and exercise, there must also be a partner who is always, at the very least, in sight. A lone horse is never happy and keeping a herd animal such as a horse on its own is also a welfare issue.

The horse owner should place particular emphasis on secure fencing for the paddock or field. Depending on the size of the stallion, the fence must be at least 1.5 metres high, or much higher for large stallions and talented jumpers. You must also use materials that are safe and easily visible for the horse. Barbed wire, stock fencing and fences made of metal wire only are totally unsuitable! Wide electric tape is suitable for fencing a large, grassy field. For stallions in particular, small paddocks should be surrounded with sturdy wood or metal fences, additionally secured with electric fencing. It goes without saying that the fence must be checked regularly to ensure that it can protect against break-outs!

If two horses sniff each other with curiosity and interest like this, a wonderful friendship could develop.
(Photo: Ostwald)

The **right partner** for the stallion

We have already mentioned several times that the stallion should be allowed direct contact with at least one other horse or pony, if possible. But which horses are suitable? A tolerant gelding is usually uncomplicated. It is also entirely possible to keep a stallion with a mare, providing that the mare is already pregnant or is not in season at the time (the pair must be separated when the mare is in season). Because of these limiting factors, the decision for a gelding is obvious. Stallion plus stallion can also work well, as we will describe in a moment.

So how do you spot the right partner for your stallion? In the case of high-ranking, strong and dominant stallions, a quiet gelding that will accept the stallion as a leader and willingly submit is the best choice. It is possible to keep low-ranking, reserved (less stallion-ish) stallions, that are willing to submit, with another stallion.

It is very important to assess your own stallion and the equine partner in question thoroughly. For this, you will need good observational skills and some experience with horses. If you are not quite sure, you should seek advice from an expert. The trained eye of an expert will help with the decision as to whether to risk trying to introduce them to each other. If possible, this professional should also be there when the horses meet for the first time.

Nothing should be rushed during the first meeting of the potential field mates. We advise against simply putting both of them out into a large field together, because this can go very wrong. The best thing is to turn both horses out into adjoining fields first and observe them. If one of them behaves aggressively, perhaps kicking through the fence or ignoring it completely, you should interrupt the attempt at an introduction. If, on the other hand, the horses sniff each other quietly or ignore each other, the next step can be to leave them together in a securely fenced area. An indoor or outdoor riding arena would be suitable, for example. The area should not be too big, so that you can still intervene quickly and effectively if need be. Again, you need to watch the horses carefully. Mutual sniffing, nipping, running together while bucking and kicking out or mutual, playful "knee nipping" are completely normal behaviour where you do not need to intervene. However, if both hors-

es fly at each other with flattened ears and bared teeth or if one is cornering and chasing the other, you shouldn't assume that a harmonious partnership will result and you should end the attempt immediately.

Please remember that horses do not necessarily have to get on just because their owners are friends. Looking for a field companion among the horses of good friends is admittedly an obvious first step, but for the good of the horses you should maintain your objectivity and accept it if the "dream partnership" does not work. Friendships among horses cannot be forced.

The stallion in a **herd**

There are usually two ways of keeping herds – in open barns with access to fields or in open barns where the horses have to walk to different areas in order to access food and water. The latter just means that horses are kept together in a larger area, but not that they necessarily have free access to turnout. This system is less suitable for stallions because of the often limited space available. For that reason, we want to focus on open barn systems where there is a sufficiently large shelter and a large outdoor area. Ideally, this area will, in turn, be divided into resting areas, exercise areas and eating areas, which gives the horses a reason to move around a lot. It is important to have plenty of space, especially when integrating a stallion into this kind of open barn system, otherwise there will be quarrels. It is

Stallions can also be kept in a herd, if enough space is available. (Photo: Slawik)

important that the stallion is well social-ised and that you can accurately assess his behaviour. If he is a horse that tends to assume a high-ranking position, you should make sure that he does not run straight into the highest-ranking horse when you try to integrate him into the herd. If, on the other hand, he is a rather submissive animal, you should not throw him in at the deep end by putting him straight into the existing herd. In both cases, you should initially select an appropriate partner from the herd and famil-iarise both horses with each other. Gradu-ally, more and more herd members can be added until all of the horses are together. It is important that competent persons observe

the behaviour of the horses during the habit-uation period and intervene in good time in the case of any problems. A stallion can also be kept in a herd with mares if the mares are either already pregnant or are supposed to be covered by this stallion. Otherwise, a "men only" herd is the better choice. The simplest and safest version is a group of geldings with one stallion. You cannot make sweeping generalisations about whether several stallions can be kept together in a herd. It can work, but if you want to try it, you will have to know the horses and be able to assess them very well. In the case of several stallions, or more rarely, stallion-ish geldings, in a herd, you should re-

*For some horses, life in a herd equals stress and they
will be happier with a single horse as a partner.
(Photo: Ostwald)*

member that the mere presence of mares, even if they are not permanently in view but only occasionally ridden past the paddock or field, can lead to rivalry. The environment in which the open barn system is situated therefore plays an important role.

If pure herd management in an open barn system or, during the summer, in a large field is not possible, a combination of stable/open barn overnight and communal turn-out in a herd during the day can be a good option, although what we said above about integration into the herd applies here.

There are also cases where keeping a stallion in a herd is rather unsuitable, for example if the horses at an establishment change frequently, the associated constant changes in the herd structure and hierarchy would greatly increase the risk of injury. Keeping stallions in a herd is often not possible if the stallions are supposed to perform competitively at a high level, because it would be difficult to feed them according to their needs. Feeding systems that allow individual feeding are available, but they are very expensive and therefore not common at many yards.

Sometimes, after several attempts, you will establish that a horse simply will not integrate into a herd. It will stand on its own or even run away from its companions and life in a herd will mean a lot of stress for this horse. It is usually possible to find at least a single partner for horses like this. The absolute exception are horses for whom even this is not possible and who are actually better off alone (naturally at least with visual contact with other horses). However, the chance of owning such an exceptional case is slim. Please do not give up too hastily after a couple of tries. Perhaps you have just read your stallion wrong and an expert could help you to find the right partner for him.

Warning!

It is important to remember that stallions can behave unpredictably in herds or even with individual companions! We have already had several experiences where stallions that have coexisted calmly and peacefully with other horses have suddenly attacked, bitten or beaten up other herd members, as if a switch had been flicked. Everything then goes back to normal in the days and weeks that follow, but the behaviour can always re-occur, without any recognisable warning in advance. When the aggressive behaviour has been shown for a second time, at the latest, you have to act and try either to integrate the stallion into another herd or to find a suitable partner for him.

The stallion is stressed and still overwhelmed by his new freedom. (Photo: Ostwald)

What about unsocialised stallions that have been kept in **isolation**?

Unfortunately, we cannot take for granted that the types of management described above are suitable for all stallions. So what do you do with an older stallion that has been kept in isolation and without turn-out for years and that has lost any social skills as a result? Here, we will describe a method that has worked well for us.

To begin with, put the stallion in a habituation stable, i.e. a stable with bars that are three to four centimetres apart. There should be a tolerant and inconspicuous gelding in each of the stables to the right and left of the stallion's stable. This means that the stallion can see and sniff the other horses, but the narrow bars will prevent him from getting caught and injuring himself if he rears. It goes without saying that the dividing walls must also be high enough that the stallion cannot get his front legs over them.

At the same time, the stallion should also be habituated to regular turn-out. To begin with, it is best to turn the stallion out in a lungeing pen with a high fence, after training or warming up on the horse walker. This helps to prevent the stallion from getting carried away with his new-found freedom and even injuring himself with excessive horseplay. Stallions will usually soon become more balanced as a result of regular training and turn-out, which will help with their socialisation.

When you can tell that the presence of other horses will no longer cause the stallion any stress, the next step is to open up a small hole in the bars on the side of the preferred neighbour. Now the stallion can make direct contact. In the best case, it will work straight away and both neighbours will meet amicably and groom each other. However, in the worst case, the stallion can bite the gelding's neck. In order to avoid the latter, the stallion should be held by an experienced person, who can intervene quickly if required, during the first attempts at contact.

If the stallion has become used to regular turn-out in the lungeing pen and later in a paddock or field and if contact with other horses no longer poses a problem, you can try putting him out in a field or turn-out area with another horse, as described in the section "The right partner for the stallion".

Anatomy and
health

Healthy, shiny and powerful. This is how we want our stallions to be. (Photo: Slawik)

In order to cover stallions as thoroughly as possible in this book, we still need to provide information about stallion anatomy and to explain about stallion health, or rather, diseases that are typical of stallions. We also want to explain the hygiene measures that should be taken in stallions and how to perform them.

The **sexual organs** of the stallion

Stallions have internal and external sexual organs. The internal sexual organs are the testes and the epididymis, the accessory glands, i.e. vesicular gland, prostate gland and bulbourethral gland, as well as the glandular part of the deferent duct (ampulla of the deferent duct) and the spermatic cord, while the external sexual organs are the penis and scrotum.

The testicles are oval in shape and, in German Warmblood stallions, have an average total weight of 300 grams. They continue to grow until sexual maturity has been reached (at the age of around 15 months). The testes

A diagram of the sexual organs of the stallion.
(Diagram: Retsch-Amschler)

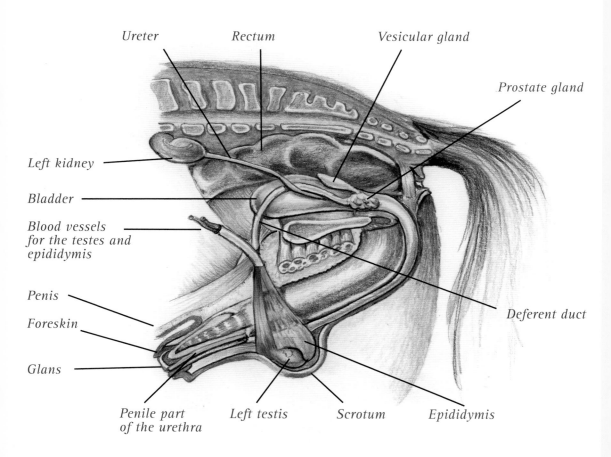

Ureter — Rectum — Vesicular gland — Prostate gland — Left kidney — Bladder — Blood vessels for the testes and epididymis — Penis — Foreskin — Glans — Penile part of the urethra — Left testis — Scrotum — Epididymis — Deferent duct

require a lower temperature than that inside the abdominal cavity in order to be able to produce sperm, which is why they are outside, but nevertheless protected in the scrotum. The optimum temperature of the testes is 33 degrees Celsius and infertility may result if the temperature falls well below or greatly exceeds this level. A mechanism for temperature regulation exists for that reason. If the temperature outside is very low, the cremaster muscle tenses, drawing the testes closer to the body. If the temperature is too high, this muscle relaxes and the testes move away from the body, back to their normal position. The cremaster muscle is also affected by movement. When the stallion moves, he tenses his back and abdominal muscles and therefore also the cremaster muscle, which raises the testes. The muscle relaxes again when the stallion is relaxed.

The scrotum is made up of several layers. Its inner wall is an evagination of the peritoneum that is described as a vaginal tunic in the area of the scrotum. The inguinal ring is a tendinous hole between the abdominal muscles and the point where the scrotum connects to the abdominal cavity. A testis consists of many small, closely interwoven spermatic tubules where the precursors of sperm (spermatozoa) are formed. The spermatic tubules run bundled into the head of the epididymis where the spermatozoa mature into sperm. By the time they reach the epididymal duct, they have achieved motility. The sperm reach the urethra via the deferent duct. In the urethra, there are three different types of genital glands whose secretions act as growth media for the sperm, together with which they form the semen.

The secretions maintain the motility of the sperm and therefore its ability to fertilise. In addition to sperm production, the testes are also responsible for the formation of the male sex hormone, testosterone. Testosterone is produced in all horses, but in stallions, higher quantities of it are produced in the Leydig cells of the testicles and in the adrenal glands. In geldings, much smaller quantities of testosterone are produced in the adrenal glands only and in mares, small quantities are produced in the ovaries. In stallions, testosterone is responsible for sperm production (spermatogenesis), libido, the formation of the sexual organs and the typical stallion appearance. In Warmbloods, a stallion's penis is around 44 cm long and has a diameter of around 5 cm. During mating, the penis is responsible for conducting semen. The body of the penis consists of two cavernous bodies that form one soft, stretchy hollow that is supplied by blood. When the stallion is aroused, these cavernous bodies become filled with more blood as the blood supply increases and blood drainage decreases. As a result, the penis grows in size and becomes stiff (doubles in length and circumference). This process, called haemodynamics, is controlled by the nerves. The penis is protected by what is known as the sheath. It acts as a protective sleeve into which the penis can be telescopically withdrawn. Glands inside the sheath release an oily substance that protects the penis and keeps it smooth. Together with flakes of dead skin and skin bacteria, it forms a yellowish to reddish-brown substance called smegma.

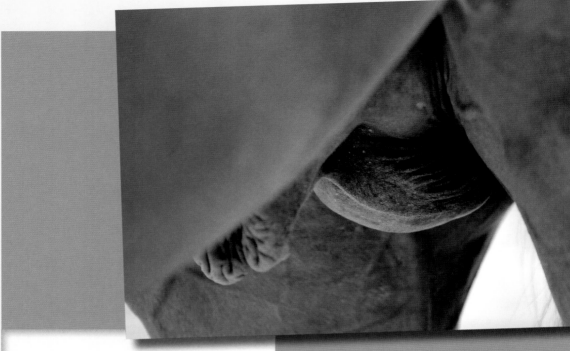

Rig

A rig is a stallion at least one of whose testes has not descended but remained in the abdominal cavity or groin. Only the external testis was removed at castration. The testis inside is usually much smaller and, because of the excessively high temperature, it cannot produce sperm capable of fertilisation. However, it will be likely to develop tumours. Rigs are also often more stallion-like in their behaviour and are more difficult to handle than geldings. For these reasons, rigs should always be fully castrated, even if it means an operation under general anaesthetic in a hospital. In the eyes of the law, selling a horse as a gelding when it is actually a rig is misrepresentation.

This photograph shows a rig. The incompletely descended testes can clearly be seen.
(Photo: Ostwald)

Stallion-specific **diseases**

At this point, we would like to outline common diseases specific to stallions in the form of a table. These diseases do not just occur in stallions used for breeding. This table can only give an initial overview of symptoms and approaches to treatment and does not replace the vet under any circumstances.

Disease	Description	Symptoms	Treatment
Cryptorchidism (rig)	One or both testes did not descend into the scrotum after birth but are still in the abdomen or inguinal canal. The causes are unclear, but it may be inherited from the sire.	Undescended testes fall behind in their development. A gelding may continue to show stallion behaviour as a result of the undescended testis. Testes that remain in the abdominal cavity have a tendency to form tumours.	The hidden testis or testes are removed operatively.
Scrotal or inguinal hernia	Loops of small intestine enter the scrotum through the inguinal canal.	In mild cases, there may just be lameness in the hindquarters. The horse will show signs of colic if the intestine is trapped and the blood supply has been cut off. The testis is much bigger on one side and usually very painful.	Emergency! The stallion must be operated on immediately in a clinic. Time is of the essence, even if the horse has so far only shown mild symptoms, because parts of the intestine become necrotic very quickly if circulation is poor.
Inflammation of the testes (orchitis)	Inflammation of the testes is usually caused by injury (during covering, for example) or viral or bacterial infections.	Solid and very painful swelling of one or both testes.	Hosing with cold water, anti-inflammatory drugs and, if necessary, antibiotics.
Spermiostasis (plugged ampullae)	Often the result of inflammation of the testes (see above). "Old" sperm accumulate in the tail of the epididymis and in the deferent duct.	Very high sperm density in the ejaculate with a high number of dead sperm and clumps made up of semen and dead sperm.	Collection of semen twice a day for several days, combined with administration of hormones.

Disease	Description	Symptoms	Treatment
Paraphimosis (prolapse)	The stallion is no longer able to retract his penis once he has let it down. Can be caused by injuries, tumours or nerve-related prolapse of the penis.	The stallion does not retract his penis. Abrasions or inflammation may occur. The penis hangs down limply and swells up distinctly within a few hours.	Cleaning the sheath, trying to put the penis back in manually, as well as movement, massage, hosing with cold water and salves may help. If risk of injury is present, for example from kicks or when standing up, it can be reduced by tying up the penis.
Tumours on the penis	Tumours are usually located around the tip of the penis. Risk factors are old age, light-skinned genitals, increased formation of smegma and inadequate hygiene.	Tumours, especially around the tip of the penis, often with a cauliflower-like shape, that are only recognisable when the penis is let down. In some cases, the tumour may make letting down the penis difficult. Foul-smelling, bloody secretion often flows out of the sheath.	An operation to remove the tumour must be performed immediately. Partial amputation of the penis is often necessary for complete removal.

Venereal diseases

Disease	Description	Symptoms	Treatment
Dourine	Often deadly infection with protozoan parasites Trypanosoma equiperdum. Spread through coitus and found all over the world. Both genders are affected.	Two to twelve weeks after infection, redness, swellings and blisters will appear on the whole of the penis and slimy discharge will be visible at the urethra and on the glans. The blisters may turn into ulcers.	Notifiable disease! Treatment may be attempted in a clinical setting if the disease is spotted early enough (swab sample 14 days before covering).

Disease	Description	Symptoms	Treatment
		Later, weals appear on the neck, shoulders, lower chest and croup. Lameness may occur (primarily in the hindquarters) because of nerve damage.	Intensive treatment over several weeks is very costly and must be approved by the public authorities. Neither stallions nor mares may be used for breeding again, even after successful treatment.
CEM (contagious equine metritis)	Infectious, bacterial inflammation of the uterus in mares that is transmitted by the stallion (or by con-taminated hands and instruments during artificial insemination). The pathogen is Taylorella equigenitalis.	The stallion is asymptomatic but passes on the pathogen during coitus. In mares, there will be slimy, foul-smelling vaginal discharge, lowered fertility and spontane-ous abortion.	Prevention: swab samples before and during the covering season. Treatment: daily, thorough washing of the penis and foreskin with special disinfectant solutions, antibiotics.
Genital horse pox (equine coital exanthema)	A benign genital infection caused by equine herpes virus 3 (EHV-3). It is transmitted during coitus.	Three to twelve days after infection, blisters or pustules, which can be up to the size of a pea, appear on the penis or foreskin. General condition is normally undisturbed. Mares will also have pustules in the genital area. Vaginal discharge is often present because of additional bacteria.	The infection subsides within one to two weeks. The horse will then be healthy again, but will remain a life-long carrier of the disease and may never be used for breeding again. Inoculation is not possible.

Disease	Description	Symptoms	Treatment
Equine viral arteritis (EVA)	Globally distributed viral infection (arterivirus). Transmitted nasally, through feed or through coitus or artificial insemination. A high proportion of all horses carry this virus but do not become ill. In stallions, the virus persists in the accessory genital glands.	Inflammation of the lymph and blood vessels will occur two to ten days after infection. This leads to fever, apathy, oedema (especially of the limbs) or reddening of the mucous membranes (especially in the eyes).	Notifiable disease! No anti-viral treatment for EVA exists, so it must be treated purely symptomatically. Prevention: blood test of stud stallions before the covering season. Infected stallions and mares are excluded from breeding.

Clean the sheath and penis carefully using a mild disinfectant solution. (Photo: Ostwald)

Hygiene is the best prevention

We have now described the most important illnesses that you, as a stallion owner, should know about and be able to recognise. To spare the stallion the unpleasantness of infections or not being able to let down the penis because of poor hygiene, the extended penis should be regularly cleaned. Many stallions do not like this procedure and will very quickly retract their penis on contact. If this is the case, you should take advantage of the horse being under sedation for his dental examination, which should take place at least once a year. When under sedation, the stallion will often let down his penis by himself and, if not, it is easy to manually pull the penis out of the sheath when the horse is relaxed. Now the penis and sheath can be carefully cleaned with lukewarm water, a mild disinfectant solution (especially for mucous membranes) and a sponge. This is safe for the owner and not uncomfortable for the horse. Other cleaning products such as shampoos are not recommended because they could irritate the sensitive genital area.

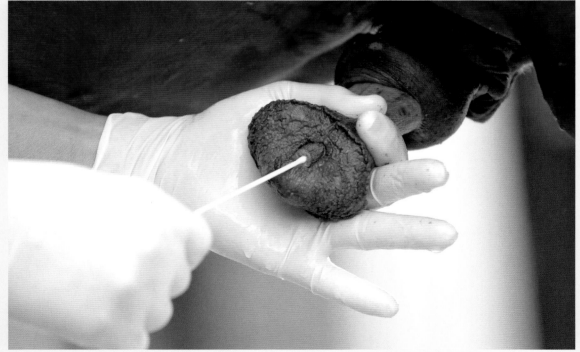

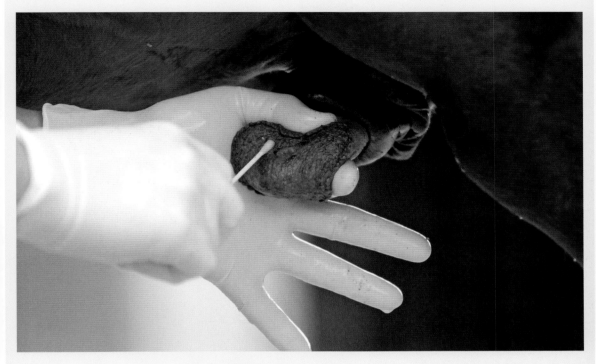

In stallions, swab samples are taken from the shaft of the penis, the urethra and the urethral fossa. (Photos: Ostwald)

Taking swab samples

Taking swab samples is a job for a vet or other specialist such as an insemination technician. Nevertheless, it is interesting for stallion owners to at least be familiar with the procedure. Swab samples are compulsory for all stallions before the breeding season so that diseases can be spotted in time and mares can be protected against the infectious ones. Swab samples are an important tool for diagnosing diseases even in stallions that are not used for breeding.

Three swab samples are taken: from the shaft of the penis, from the urethra and one from the urethral fossa. Genitals must not have been cleaned just before collecting the sample, because this could distort the result. It can be helpful to take swabs from a sexually aroused stallion because otherwise it is not easy to reach the three desired areas. A nearby in-season mare will make the procedure easier. The samples must reach the laboratory within 48 hours, chilled and packaged in special culture media.

The pros and cons of keeping a stallion

You can have a lot of fun with a stallion that has been well trained and managed in a species-appropriate way. (Photo: Slawik)

This book is not just intended to be a guide for stallion owners, but to help everybody who is new to the topic of stallion owning to decide for or against a stallion. So, to finish, we want to go into the pros and cons again.

Which **person** is right for a stallion?

A basic requirement for keeping a stallion should be years of experience with horses and, for everybody who wants not only to breed from but also to ride their stallion, solid ridden experience is obviously also important. Stallions are not for beginners! Mental fitness is particularly important when dealing with stallions and a stallion owner needs to be consistent and assertive. Owners have to think ahead and be able to quickly assess situations and deal with them appropriately. Anxiety or uncertainty have no place here and could even be dangerous.

Gaining a little experience with stallions before you fulfil your desire for one of your own is highly recommended. You may be able to find a horse to share or benefit from the experiences of other liveries or friends. It makes sense for your first stallion to be well-trained and well-mannered. If you have even considered it in the first place, taking on a difficult stallion that needs to be retrained first should be "saved" as a challenge for later on. If, due to lack of time, you cannot look after your stallion by yourself, you must remember that anybody who helps to exercise or look after your horse must have adequate experience with stallions.

At this point, we would like to emphasise again that, as a stallion owner, you are responsible for species-appropriate management. If the stable yards available in your area mean that you could only keep a stallion by himself and without adequate turn-out or if you cannot find a yard with staff who are experienced with stallions and with suitable training facilities, you should not buy a stallion.

(No) Status symbol?

What horse-lover has not dreamed of owning his or her own stallion? But no matter how beautiful and impressive you may find stallions and no matter how much respect, attention and wonder an animal like this could bring you, if species-appropriate management and competent handling are not guaranteed, the dream of a stallion should remain a dream, for the good of the horse!

The practical **benefits** of a stallion

We have again pointed out the problems of stallion ownership and the special requirements that stallions place on their owners. There are obviously advantages to stallions too, but you can only enjoy them when everything works regarding management and handling.

The male hormones, especially testosterone, create an attractive, sporty appearance. In comparison with geldings and mares, stallions usually build muscle more quickly and easily. The muscles are particularly well defined just where we like to see them

The shiny coat, which is caused by hormones, gives
stallions a very special charisma. (Photo: Slawik)

on sports horses – on the neck and back. By their very nature, stallions always look wonderful and fit. Bone density also increases more quickly in stallions and hormones cause the epiphyseal plates (growth plates between the bones and joints) to close earlier so that stallions mature faster than geldings. Stallions tend to stand in a compact square shape, whereas geldings tend to be rectangular. Stallions also have shinier and usually shorter coats than geldings or mares. They require less grooming and clipping is often not necessary in the winter.

This means that a stallion will make an impression in the dressage arena or at shows more easily than a gelding or a mare. However, even the noblest appearance cannot mask poor basic paces, bad riding or a lack of basic training.

In the best case, a stallion will not just cost money, but make money. Obviously, this is only the case if he has good qualities as a sire and if there is the corresponding demand. The stud fee is determined by the stallion owner in agreement with the breed association and may vary greatly, depending on quality, success and profile of a Warmblood stallion. In purebred stallions, it may be considerably more.

Although definitely not a deciding factor for keeping a stallion, but more of a practical "side effect", stallions' marking behaviour makes mucking out easier. Most stallions dung almost exclusively in a certain corner of their stable, paddock or field. This saves walking great distances to collect muck and the tiresome separation of bedding and dung becomes almost completely unnecessary.

When is **castration** appropriate?

Stallions are normally castrated at a young age if it has already become clear that they are not suitable for breeding and are very likely to have an easier and more species-appropriate life as geldings. Geldings that have been castrated early are usually much larger than they would have been as stallions because the growth plates close later in geldings. In sports horses in particular, this has the positive side effect of making buyers easier to find. A stallion that has turned out to be too small for breeding (height limits do exist) will clearly be more difficult to sell than a slightly larger, well-trained gelding.

English Thoroughbreds are the exception. Because their careers as racehorses begin very early and because they qualify as breeding stallions not through tests but on the basis of their origins and racing performance, they remain stallions initially so that they can be used for breeding if they are successful.

The optimum age at which a young stallion should be castrated is a question of judgement and it is not possible to make sweeping generalisations. Some horse owners have their young stallions castrated as soon as the testes have fully descended, before they even reach sexual maturity. The reason is that they do not have the option of taking their colt foal to a pure stallion yard, and castration lets them give their horse a species-appropriate life with other horses of different genders. Some owners wait until the age of two to three years, or even

Usually only geldings are allowed to coexist in a herd. These management conditions are more difficult to create for stallions. (Photo: Ostwald)

longer. This, in turn, has the "advantage" of less growth in terms of size, and the development of a typical stallion appearance. A stallion herd may be available in which a young stallion can be reared, and castration will therefore only be necessary when work begins. The breeder may first want to see how a good colt foal develops so that he can be presented for grading if appropriate. On the whole, the following applies. The earlier a horse is castrated, the better he will normally cope with the procedure, with regard to anaesthesia, wound healing and strength of the immune system.

All horses become nervous or excited at some point.
However, if it becomes a permanent state for a stallion,
you should consider castration. (Photo: Ostwald)

However, if the stallion is healthy, it is basically possible to have him anaesthetised at any age. The stability of the cardiovascular system and the general health of the animal influence the degree of risk of the operation to a large extent. Late castration is therefore associated with a greater risk. Wound healing may be worse, it may take longer for wounds to heal and the anaesthetic is sometimes less well tolerated. Where possible, older animals should be lying down for castration to minimise the risk of bowel prolapse.

Castration, even of an older stallion, certainly makes sense if a species-appropriate life would otherwise not be possible for the horse. For example, if it turns out that the stallion is constantly unsettled and on-edge in the presence of mares, possibly even at risk of injuring himself in the stable or breaking out from the field and covering mares, this long-term strain is intolerable for owner and animal. Stallions that turn out to be difficult to handle and aggressive and that pose a risk to riders and everybody else who deals with them also have a better prospect of a contented life as geldings.

Castration is medically necessary if the horse's health is at risk. For example, this applies to horses with cryptorchidism, because the testicle concealed in the abdominal cavity has a tendency to develop tumours. If inheritable diseases such as cryptorchidism or testicular hypoplasia (which describes a rare, sometimes congenital incomplete development of the testes) are found in stallions, they are excluded from breeding. A stallion with this kind of disease should be castrated for the simple reason of preventing him from inadvertently passing on this defect in an "accident" in the field.

From stallion to gelding – things change

The rather uncomplicated nature of geldings can be explained by the lower level of testosterone in their bodies. However, it can take different lengths of time for the stallion to become a typical gelding after castration, depending on the age at which he was castrated. As a rule, we can assume that the age in months at the time of castration is also the time that it will take for a complete change in behaviour to happen. However, there are exceptions here. It depends on the animal in question and on the environment, for example on the close proximity of mares. Experience has shown that it takes longer for stallion behaviour to stop in a mixed herd than in a same-sex herd. If an older stallion that shows very pronounced stallion behaviour is castrated, castration will not necessarily achieve the desired result. The horse will be infertile and the testosterone level will decrease but the repertoire of stallion behaviour is already so deeply entrenched that it won't just disappear and may quite possibly be maintained for the rest of the horse's life.

Mentally, older horses also cope with castration without difficulty. It goes without saying that there are physical changes. The pronounced musculature, especially on the neck and hindquarters, which is typical of stallions, usually decreases slightly. The coat may appear a little rougher and longer and

the menopause) have not been observed in horses.

This attractive gelding is clearly not a stallion. In particular, he lacks the musculature on the neck, but also the typical stallion appearance. (Photo: Slawik)

the horse will usually seem a little quieter on the whole. However, hormone-deficiency symptoms caused by castration, for example with an effect on mental wellbeing (comparable with depression in women during

> *The German word for a gelding is Wallach. Wallach was originally the word for a castrated horse that came from Wallachia in Romania. Castration became common practice early on in Eastern Europe and "Wallache" were exported from there, so the name spread and was later adopted to mean a castrated horse.*

Castration methods

Castration means complete removal of the testes, as a result of which production of sperm is no longer possible and the horse becomes infertile. Behaviour also changes because the main production sites of the male hormone testosterone are removed. Infertility can also be achieved through sterilisation, where only the deferent duct is severed. However, this method is not commonly used for horses because the testes are not removed and no change in hormones takes place, with no corresponding change in behaviour. With regard to maintenance and handling, it does not improve anything for the horse.

There are two different methods of castration that can be performed on a standing (open method under sedation and with local anaesthetic) or lying horse (open or closed method under general anaesthetic).

In order to perform a closed castration at the horse's own yard, the horse must first be anaesthetised in a quiet place. One person assists the vet, while somebody else holds the back leg out of the way.

How the extracted testis is tied off.
(Photos: Slawik)

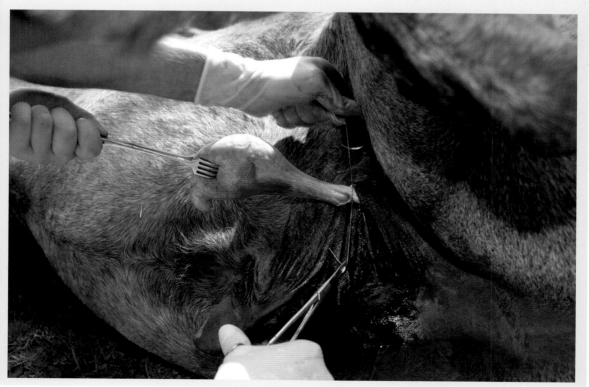

For the open method on a standing horse, the stallion is first given a sedative and then a local anaesthetic in the area of the testes. The entire operation site (lower abdomen, back legs, sexual organs and tail) is washed and disinfected with sterile solution. All of the layers of the scrotum are then opened right down to the testes with two incisions, which involves an opening in the abdominal cavity. The spermatic cord is then exposed and clamped with special castration forceps. The forceps squash the blood vessels, which usually prevents severe postoperative haemorrhage. The testis is then removed. The outer skin stays open and you must make sure that the edges of the wound do not close too early so that any secretions that form can flow away.

This method is comparatively simple and inexpensive. The risk posed by a general anaesthetic can also be avoided. However, it should also be mentioned that the risk for the vet is relatively high with this method, because he or she has to work under the horse's stomach. Even a sedated horse can be unpredictable. Haemorrhaging from the spermatic cords cannot be entirely ruled out as a possible complication of this operation. In addition, there is a relatively small risk of a prolapse of the intestine, where the loops of the intestine may reach the outside through the hole that has been created in the abdominal cavity. A prolapse of the intestine is almost always fatal.

In the case of closed castration, the stallion is placed under general anaesthetic. Nowadays it is usually performed in a clinic under sterile conditions, but it can also be done in a clean stable or a grassy field.

To begin with, the stallion is fully anaesthetised and moved onto his back or side. Following additional local anaesthesia of the genital area and surgical washing and disinfection of the operation site, the scrotum is opened, but not fully. The last layer, the vaginal tunic, remains closed. The spermatic cord and its blood vessels are tied off with resorbable (dissolving) thread and only then is the testis removed. The skin of the scrotum may also be stitched up with resorbable thread. Tying off the spermatic cord greatly reduces the risk of haemorrhaging. Prolapse of the intestine also cannot occur because the abdominal cavity is not opened. The disadvantages of this method are the higher cost and the risk posed by the general anaesthetic. Spermatic cord fistulae caused by the ligature (tying-off) are also not uncommon. In spermatic cord fistulae, the stub of the spermatic cord swells up at the ligature point. An ulcerous infection and formation of a fistula in the area of the castration scar occur as a result. Affected horses sometimes have a stiff gait or lameness and fever is also possible. A spermatic cord fistula can only be removed surgically under general anaesthetic.

Apart from the specific complications, wound infections are also possible with both methods. Wound infections manifest themselves as a swelling of the skin and the surrounding tissue in the area of the scrotum and the sheath. It is usually a haematoma (bruise), oedema (collection of fluid in the tissue) or an accumulation of wound secretion in the wound. If the horse is not an in-patient in a clinic the vet must be called. The horse will then be treated with anti-inflammatory drugs and antibiotics. Both methods have their pros and cons. You should carefully weigh up which method to choose in consultation with your vet, who is required to give you a comprehensive explanation of the operation and the associated risks.

Cryptorchids are only castrated while in a lying position, in a clinic. In the case of inguinal cryptorchids (testis in the inguinal canal), the entire inguinal canal must be opened. In the case of abdominal cryptorchids (testis in the abdominal cavity), access is gained through the side of the abdominal wall or the flank. The cryptorchid testis is usually atrophied and difficult to find. It may even be necessary to use an endoscope to locate and eventually remove the testis from the abdominal cavity.

You should wait around two to three months, until no more fertile sperm cells are found in the body. Careful integration into the herd can then take place after the castration scar has completely healed. In the case of older stallions, a longer waiting time may be appropriate because of established stallion behaviour.

Appendix

About the **authors**

At the start of his riding career, Stefan Schneider was dedicated to showjumping and rode his first "A" courses at just eleven years old. But even in his younger years, he was fascinated by horse breeds that were still exotic in Germany at the time, such as Iberians, and styles of riding such as Western, in which he was also intensively involved. He began a degree in veterinary medicine in Berlin in 1980 and then started working for himself in 1987.

Stefan Schneider with the Zweibrücker Fit for Fun.
(Photo:Ostwald)

Now he has his own premises, Rothen-kircherhof in Kirchheimbolanden, Germany, where he runs a training yard with rehabilitation centre and equine practice, together with his partner, dressage rider Uta Gräf. Along with the medical care of equine in-patients and a mobile veterinary practice, Stefan Schneider is also responsible for training young horses: from leading, loading and lunge training, double lunge work and work on long reins to breaking-in and presentation at competitions. He has become increasingly dedicated to the riding style of Doma Vaquera and has started competing in international working equitation competitions, mostly on Iberian horses.

Steffi Birk with her German Riding Pony, Komet.

Steffi Birk started riding at nine years old and from then on spent almost all of her spare time at the stables. After her Abitur (equivalent to "A" levels) she studied for three years at a private college, graduating as an equine communication scientist. Her practical studies were primarily about species-appropriate management of horses and how their natural behaviour and instincts can be taken into consideration in modern horse training. Steffi Birk gained practical experience in training young horses at several studs where she also frequently worked with stallions.

Contact with the authors
Stefan Schneider: www.gutrothenkircherhof.de, all contact details can be found here.
Steffi Birk: steffibirk87@googlemail.com

Sources and recommended reading

Becker, Horst:
The Athletic Horse:
Building on Strengths,
Overcoming Weaknesses
Cadmos, 2010

Bolze, Daniela:
My Horse Told Me:
Everyday Communication with Your Horse
Cadmos, 2013

McGreevy, Paul:
Equine Behavior
Saunders, 2004

Roberts, Monty:
The Man Who Listens To Horses
Arrow, 1997

Wendt, Marlitt:
How Horses Feel and Think
Cadmos, 2011

Internet addresses of breed associations

American Quarter Horse Association of the UK
http://aqha.uk.com/

Arab Horse Society
www.arabhorsesociety.org

British Association for the Purebred Spanish Horse
www.bapsh.co.uk

British Hanoverian Horse Society
www.hanoverian-gb.org.uk

British Horse Society
www.bhs.org.uk

British Warmblood Breeders' Studbook
www.bwbs.co.uk/

Clydesdale Horse Society
www.clydesdalehorsesociety.com

Friesian Horse Association of Great Britain
www.fhagbi.co.uk

Icelandic Horse Society of Great Britain
www.ihsgb.co.uk/

Irish Draught Horse Breeders Association
www.idhba.ie

Lusitano Breed Society of Great Britain
www.lusobreedsociety.co.uk

Sport Horse Breeding of Great Britain
www.sporthorsegb.co.uk

Thoroughbred Breeders' Association
www.thetba.co.uk

Acknowledgements

We would like to thank the people below for the contribution that their help and advice made to this book!

For support with the text:
Birte Ostwald, H. W. Kusserow, Mareike Waidner, Franziska Görwitz, Louisa Lipek, Nina Stiller, Inga Taag, Prof. Johannes Handler, Romy Matting, Sabien Seelemeyer, Lina Delius, Annette Scherkamp, Roxana Mohr, Sascha Düskow, Nina Michalewicz, Maria Franz, Franziska Aumer

For support with the photographs:
Christophe Derré (Elevage Derré – Mas Caoudou // Montpellier Polo), Jean Paul Moureau (Elevage Moureau) 132000 Arles, Nathalie Gonfond Mas des Precheurs 13520 Maussane les Alpilles – Pferde aus der Zucht von Manuel Braga (Sociedade das Silveiras) und Manuel Jorge de Oliveira, João Paiva Brandão – Coudelaria Casal Branco – Quinta do Casal Branco in Benfica do Robatejo, Manuel Braga – Sociedade das Silveiras – Belo Jardim in Samora Correia // Bereiter Pedro Vincente, Antonio Borba Monteiro – Coudelaria Julio Borba // Santo André Lusitanos in Povoa de Santo Adrião, Gräfin Teresa von Schönborn – Coudelaria Casa Cadaval in Muge.

Index

CADMOS
HORSE GUIDES

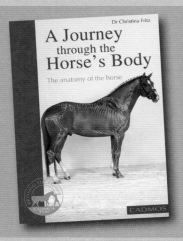

Dr Christina Fritz

A journey through the Horse's body

A fascinating journey through the horse's body! From the nostrils to the tail, the horse's organs are presented along with their structures and functions. Particular attention is paid to the musculoskeletal system. How does a horse work? What does it need to move, breathe and eat? What structures does it have and how does it use them? What mechanisms are circulation, hormonal control and reproduction based on? This book answers these and many other questions!

96 pages, Paperback
ISBN 978-0-85788-006-2

Daniela Bolze

My Horse Told Me

With their wide range of expressive behaviours, horses are always full of surprises. These behaviours can range from curious, friendly and in-secure to threatening, as a warning of attack. First and foremost, this book trains the horse lover's eye to the com-munication that constantly takes place between horses, but more importantly between people and horses in their day-to-day dealings with one another.

128 pages · Paperback
ISBN 978-0-85788-013-0

Marlitt Wendt

How Horses Feel and Think

This is a fascinating journey into the emotional world seen from a horse's point of view. The information provided offers a good basis for horse owners to learn how to relate better to their horses, to develop a more harmonious relationship to their horses and to school their horses without using force but in a positive, pro-active way.

112 pages · Paperback
ISBN 978-0-85788-000-0

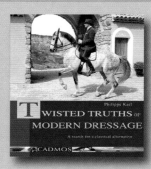

Philippe Karl

Twisted Truths of Modern Dressage

In this book, Philippe Karl, one of the most outspoken critics of the modern dressage world, reveals some disturbing facts about the physical, anatomical and mental effects through official dressage guidelines as issued by the German Horse Society (FN) on horses. By comparing these with philosophies of masters of classical riding such as La Gueriniere and Baucher, he shows possible solutions to the challenging situation of modern competitive dressage.

160 pages · Hardcover
ISBN 978-3-86127-953-2

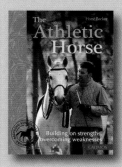

Horst Becker

The Athletic Horse

When problems occur during a horse's dressage training, all too often the question 'Why?' is igno-red. In this book, Horst Becker endeavours to find answers to this question. Whilst demonstrating ways in which a horse's weaknesses can be systematically corrected, he also shows quiet and effective ways of developing its strengths.

144 pages · Hardcover
ISBN 978-3-86127-976-1

...ore information, please visit:
...cadmos.co.uk

CADMOS